CONTENTS

ISBN-13: 978-1-4234-1788-0
ISBN-10: 1-4234-1788-7

Visit Hal Leonard Online at **www.halleonard.com**

HAL•LEONARD®
CORPORATION
7777 W. BLUEMOUND RD. P.O. BOX 13819
MILWAUKEE, WISCONSIN 53213

Against All Odds
(Take a Look at Me Now)

Words and Music by
Phil Collins

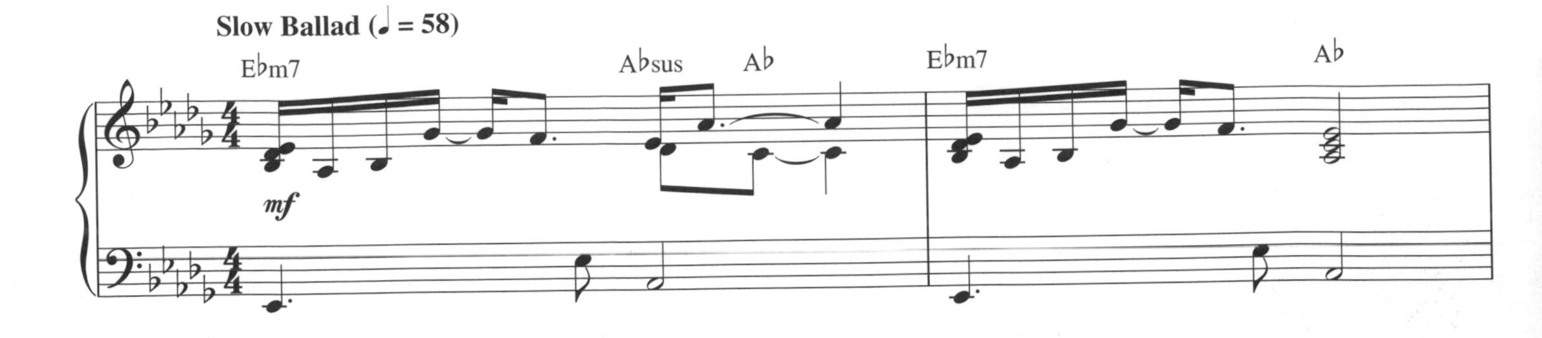

B♭m7
Cm7
D♭(add2)
E♭m7(add4)
How can you just walk a - way from me when all I can do is watch you leave? 'Cause we've

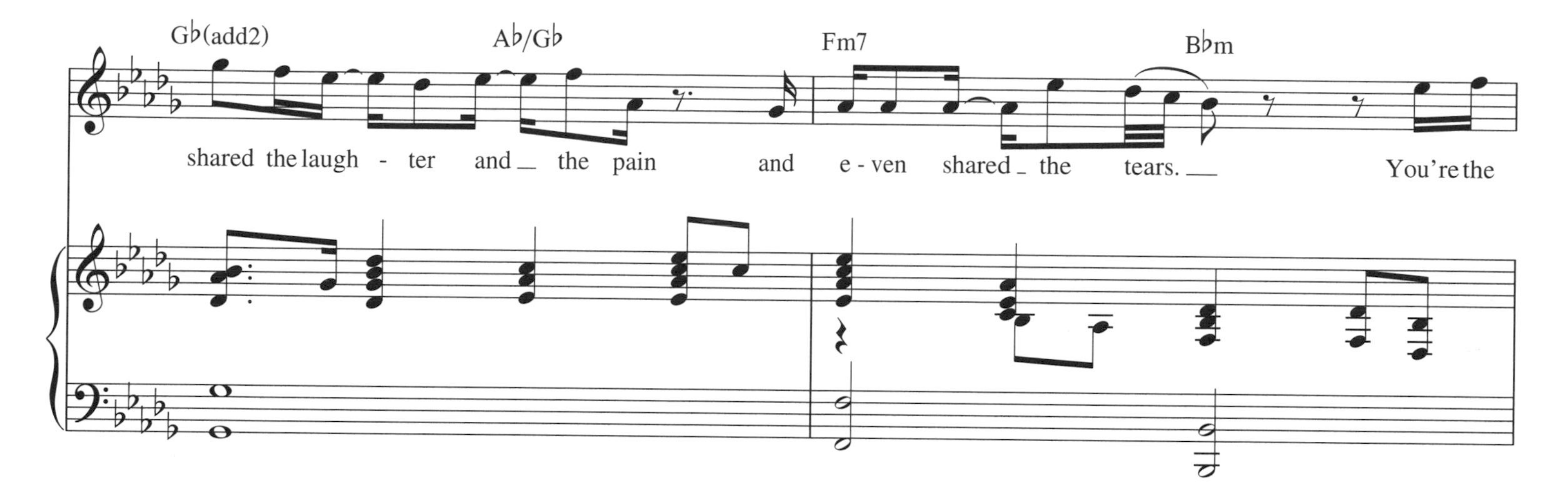
G♭(add2)
A♭/G♭
Fm7
B♭m
shared the laugh - ter and the pain and e - ven shared the tears. You're the

E♭m
A♭sus
A♭
on - ly one who real - ly knew me at all. So take a look at me now.

D♭/A♭
E♭7/A♭
Well, there's just an emp - ty space, and there's noth - ing
mf - f

B♭m
G♭
E♭m
A♭sus
left here to re-mind me, just the mem - 'ry of your face.
Ooh, take a look at me now.
Now, take a look at me now,
D♭/A♭
E♭7/A♭
Well, there's just an emp-ty space, and you com-ing back
'cause there's just an emp-ty space, but to wait
B♭m
G♭
To Coda
E♭m
to me is a-gainst the odds and that's what I've got to face.
for you is all I can do and that's what
A♭sus
A♭
I

B♭m7
Cm7
D♭(add2)
E♭m7(add4)
wish I could just make you turn a-round, turn a-round and see me cry. There's so
G♭
A♭/G♭
Fm7
B♭m
much I need to say to you, so man-y rea-sons why. You're the
E♭m
A♭sus
A♭
D.S. al Coda
on-ly one who real-ly knew me at all. So take a look at me now.
cresc.
CODA
E♭m
A♭sus
D♭/A♭
I've got-ta face. Take a good look at me now 'cause I'll still be

E♭7/A♭
B♭m
G♭
stand-ing here, and you com-ing back to me is a-gainst all odds. It's the
E♭m
A♭sus
A♭
chance I've got - ta take.
decresc.
E♭m7
A♭sus
A♭
E♭m7
A♭
Take a look at me now.
mf
E♭m7
D♭(add2)
A♭(add2)/C
G♭(add2)
A♭
molto rit.

Deacon Blues

Words and Music by Walter Becker
and Donald Fagen

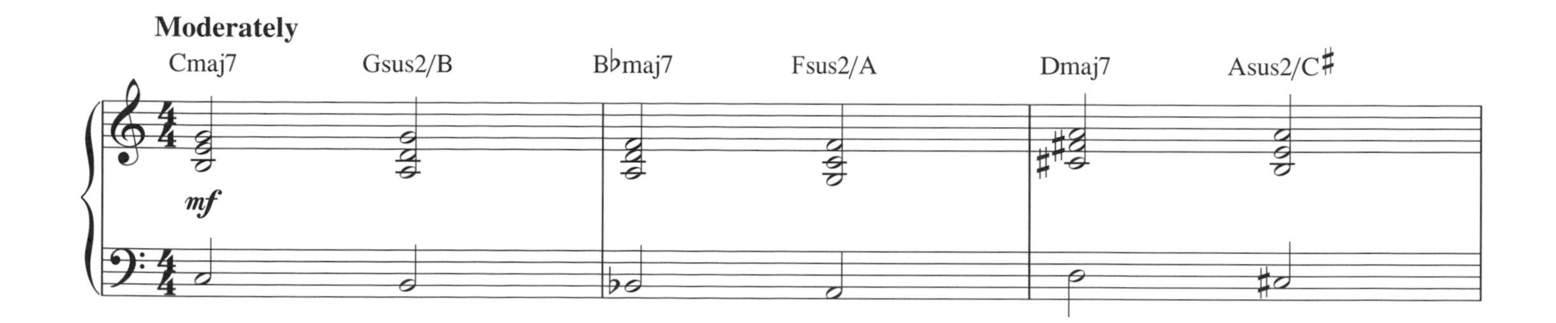
Moderately
Cmaj7
Gsus2/B
B♭maj7
Fsus2/A
Dmaj7
Asus2/C♯
mf

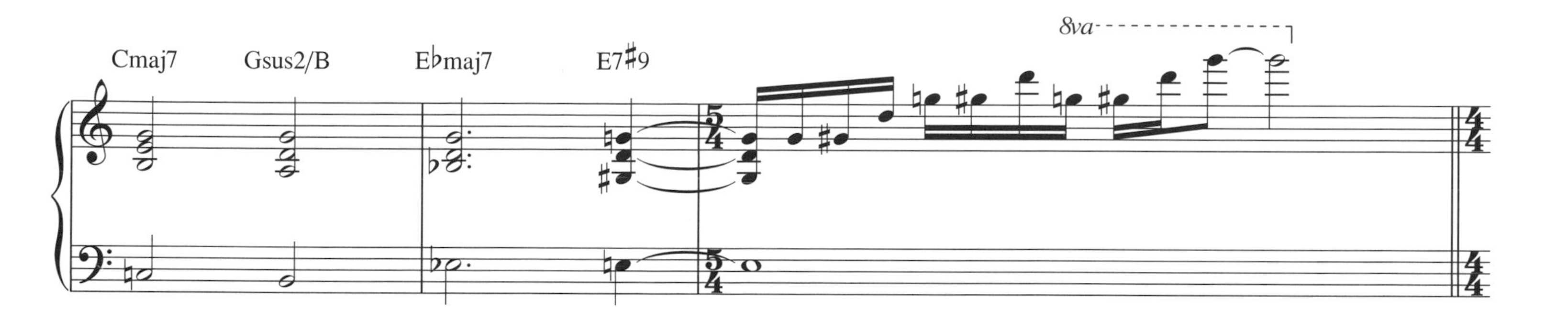
Cmaj7
Gsus2/B
E♭maj7
E7♯9
8va

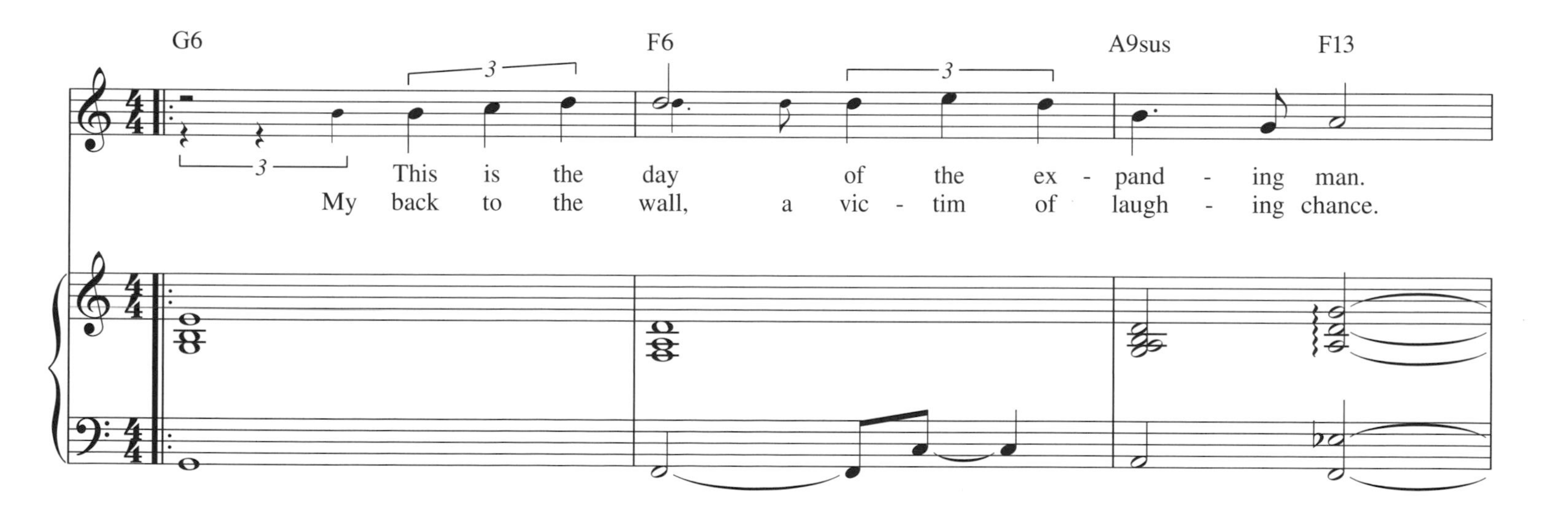
G6
F6
A9sus
F13
This is the day of the ex - pand - ing man.
My back to the wall, a vic - tim of laugh - ing chance.

G6
F6
That shape is my shade, there where I
This is for me the es - sence of

A9sus
D13
Fmaj9
used to stand.
true ro - mance.
It seems like
Shar - ing the
E7♭9
Am7
B♭13
on - ly yes - ter - day,
I gazed through the glass
at
things we know and love
with those of my kind.
Li -
E7
B7
Bm7♭5
E7
ram - blers, wild gamb - lers, that's all in the past.
ba - tions, sen - sa - tions that stag - ger the mind.
Bm11♭5
E7♯9
G13
F13
You call me a fool, you say it's a
I crawl like a vi - per through these sub -
This is the night of the ex -

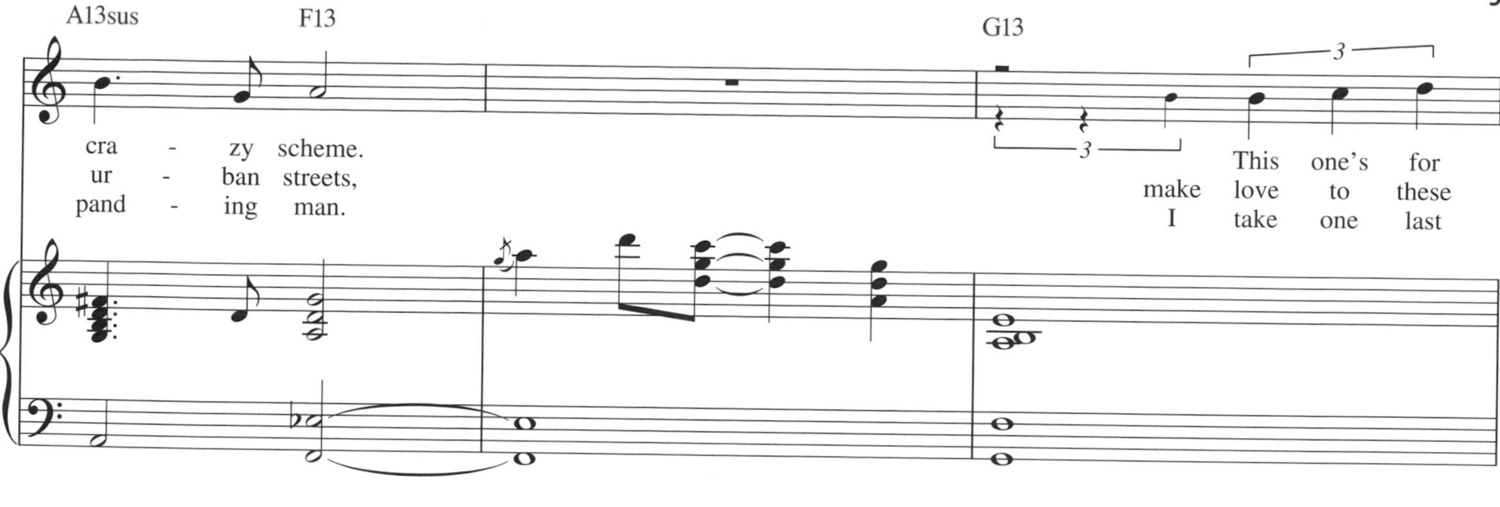
A13sus
F13
G13
3
3
cra - zy scheme. This one's for
ur - ban streets, make love to these
pand - ing man. I take one last

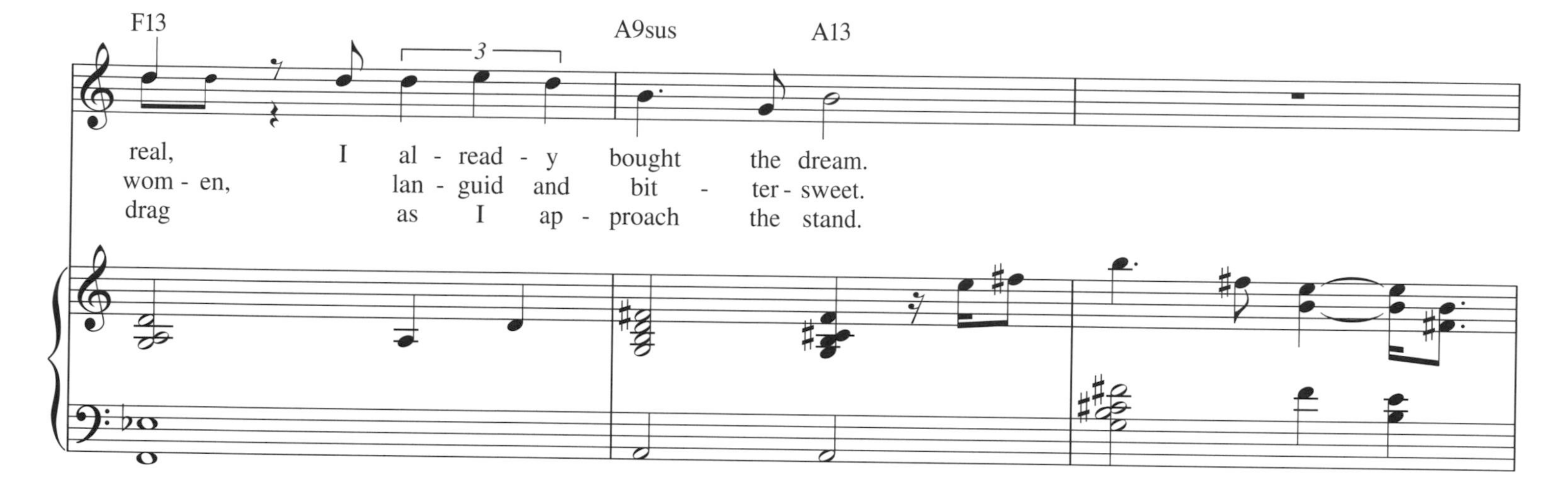
F13
A9sus
A13
3
real, I al - read - y bought the dream.
wom - en, lan - guid and bit - ter - sweet.
drag as I ap - proach the stand.

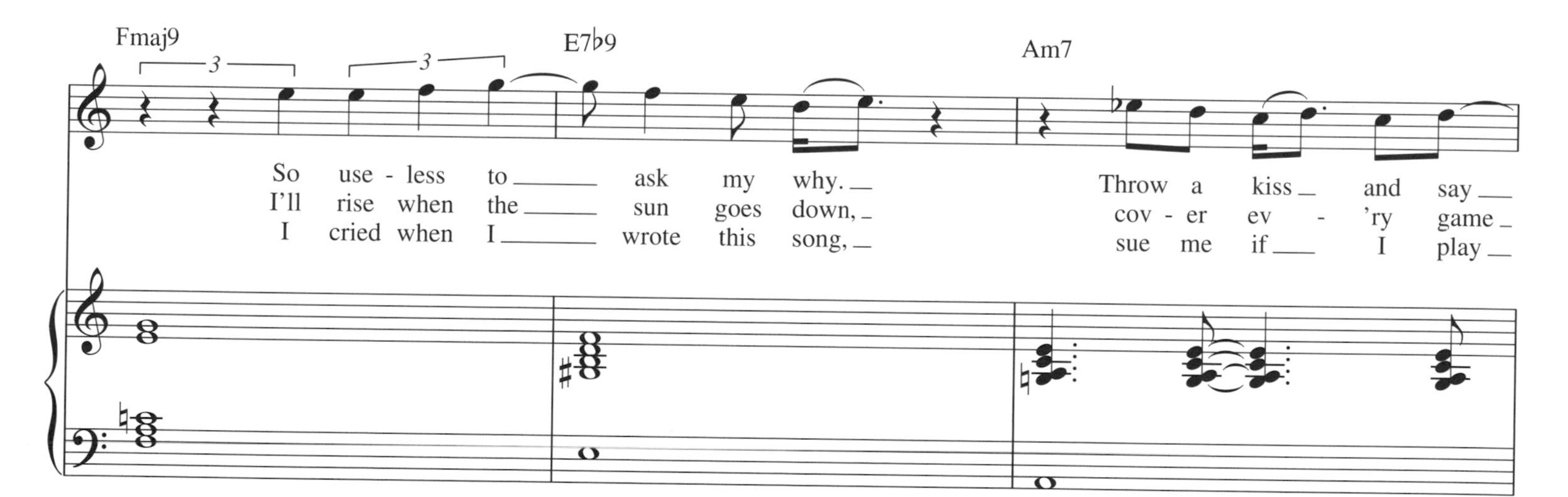
Fmaj9
E7♭9
Am7
3
3
So use - less to ask my why.
I'll rise when the sun goes down,
I cried when I wrote this song,
Throw a kiss and say
cov - er ev - 'ry game
sue me if I play

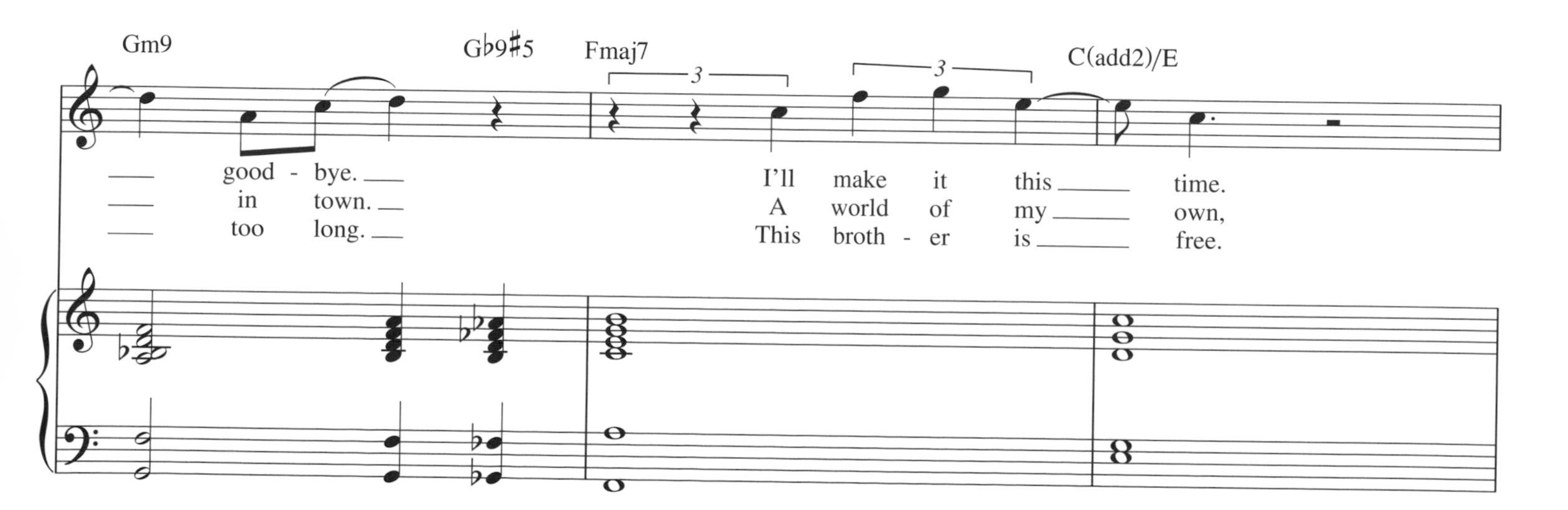
Gm9
G♭9♯5
Fmaj7
C(add2)/E
3
3
good - bye. I'll make it this time.
in town. A world of my own,
too long. This broth - er is free.

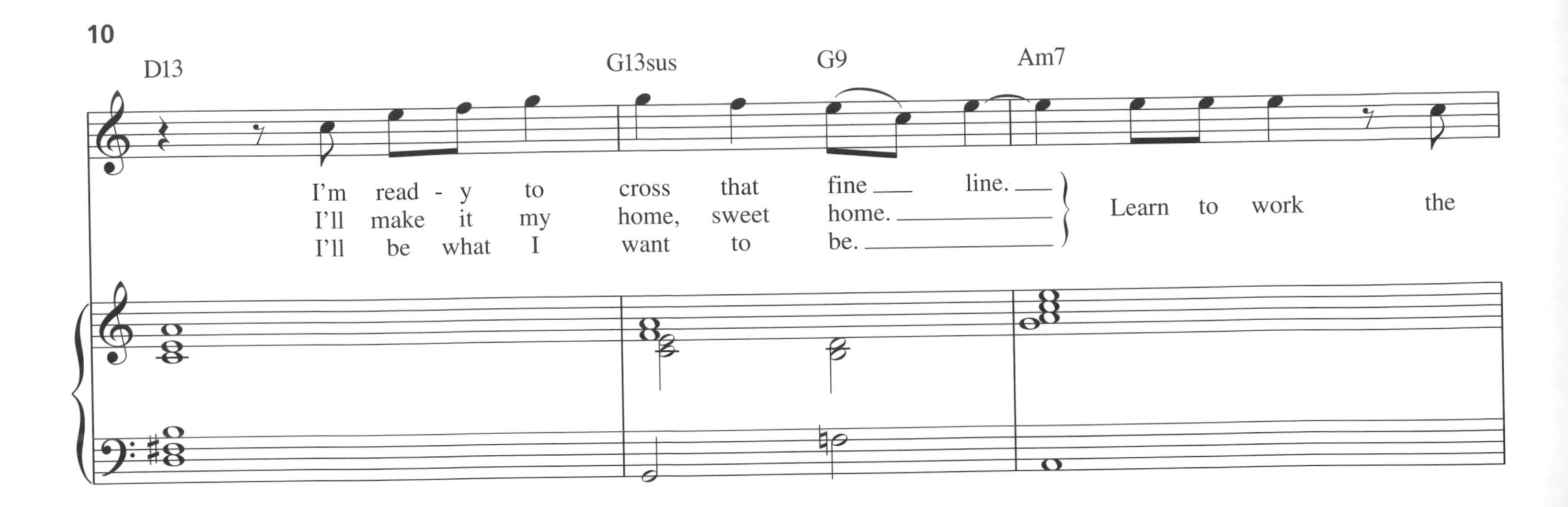
D13
G13sus
G9
Am7
I'm ready - y to cross that fine line.
I'll make it my home, sweet home.
I'll be what I want to be.
Learn to work the

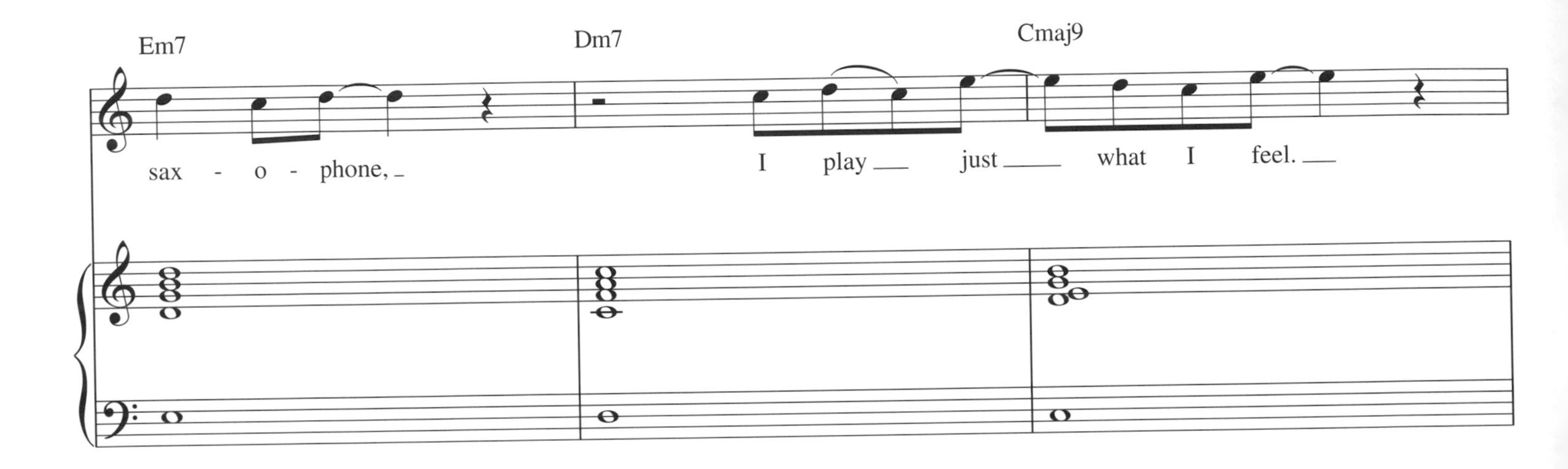
Em7
Dm7
Cmaj9
sax - o - phone,
I play just what I feel.

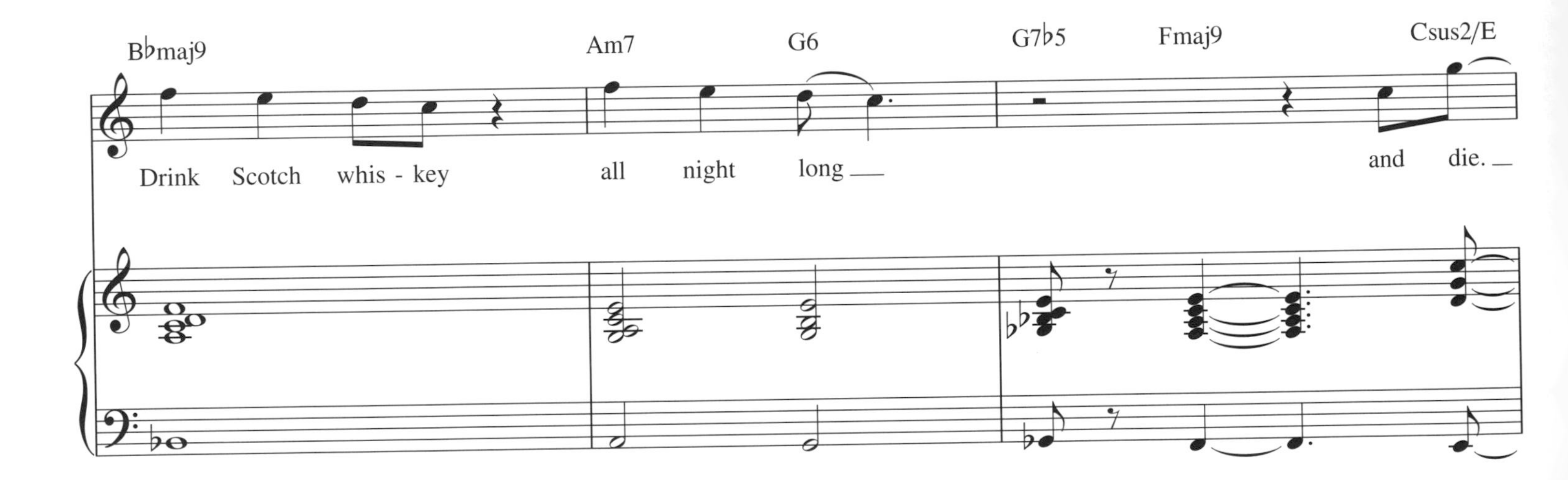
B♭maj9
Am7
G6
G7♭5
Fmaj9
Csus2/E
Drink Scotch whis - key all night long
and die.

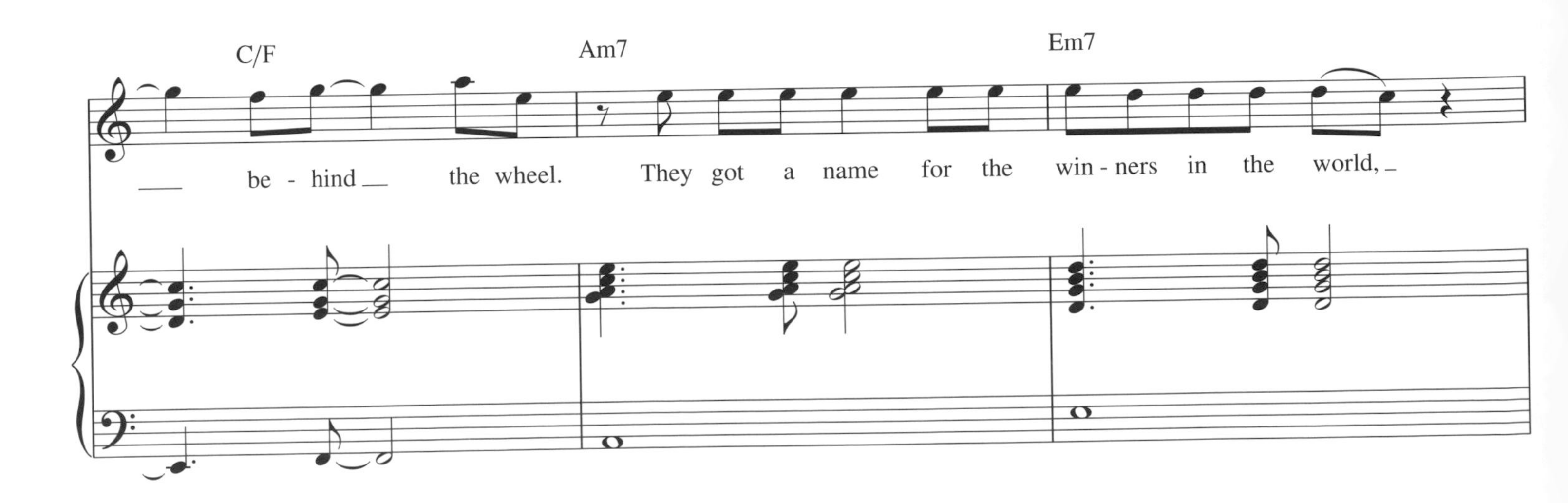
C/F
Am7
Em7
be - hind the wheel. They got a name for the win - ners in the world,

Dm7
Cmaj9
B♭maj9
I want a name when I lose. They call Al - a - bam - a the

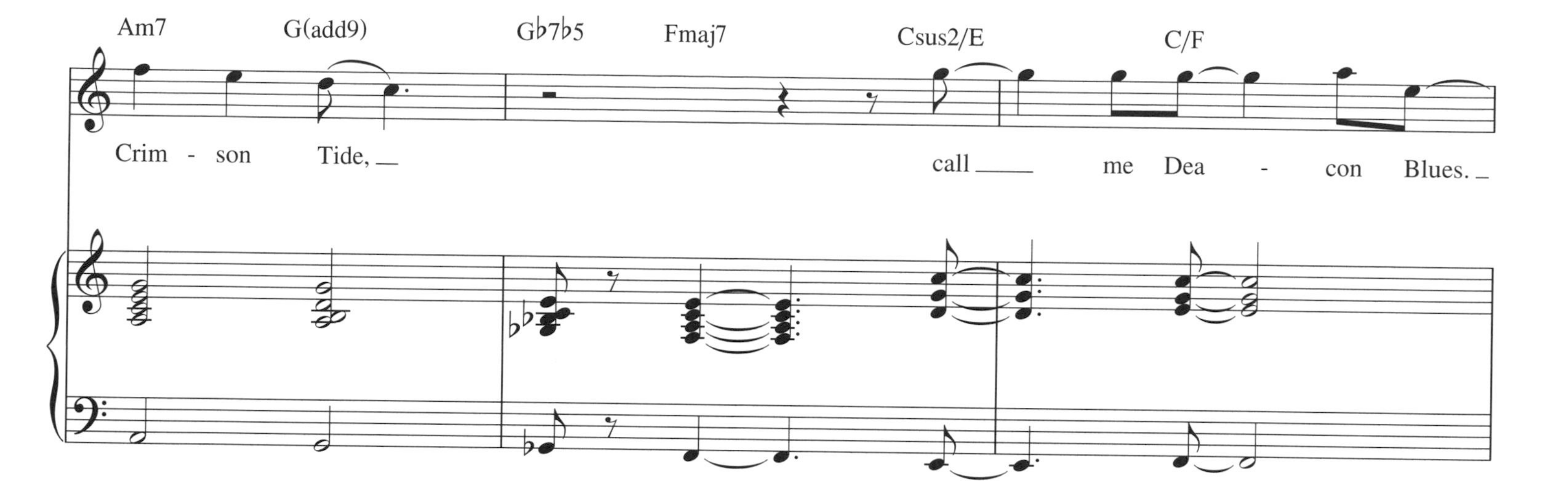
Am7
G(add9)
G♭7♭5
Fmaj7
Csus2/E
C/F
Crim - son Tide, call me Dea - con Blues.

To Coda
Am7
Em7
Dmaj7
Asus2/C♯
Cmaj9
Gsus2/B

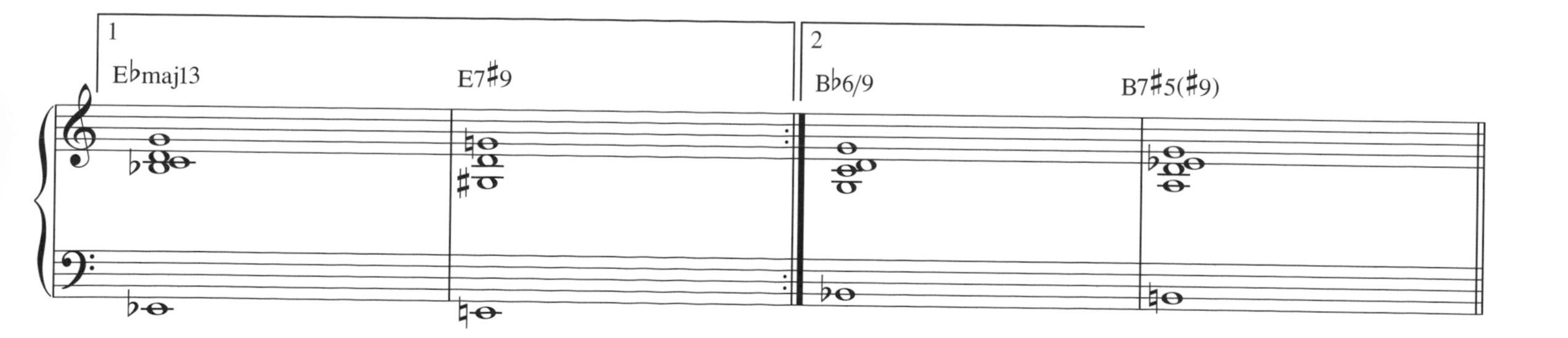
1
E♭maj13
E7♯9
2
B♭6/9
B7♯5(♯9)

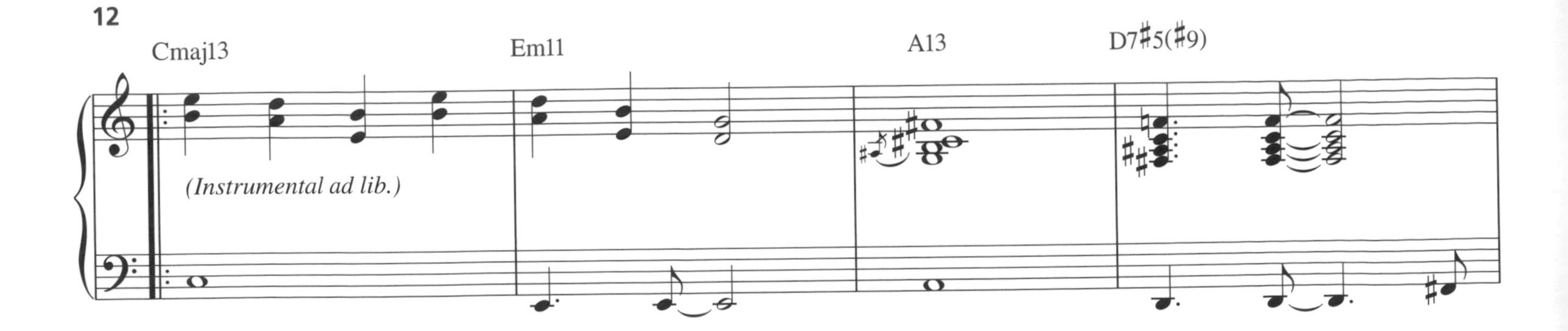
Cmaj13
Em11
A13
D7♯5(♯9)
(Instrumental ad lib.)

G13
B7♯5(♯9)
Em7

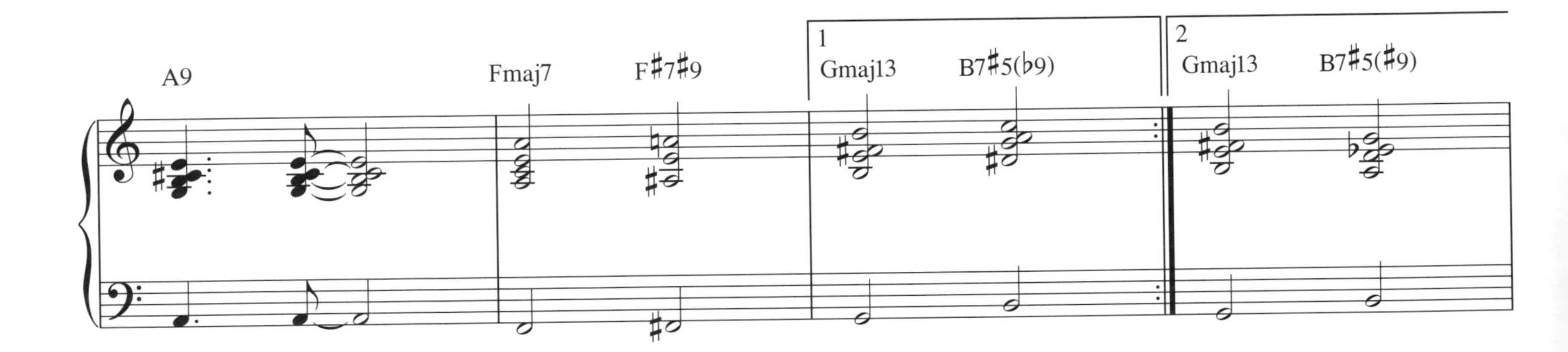
A9
Fmaj7
F♯7♯9
1
Gmaj13
B7♯5(♭9)
2
Gmaj13
B7♯5(♯9)

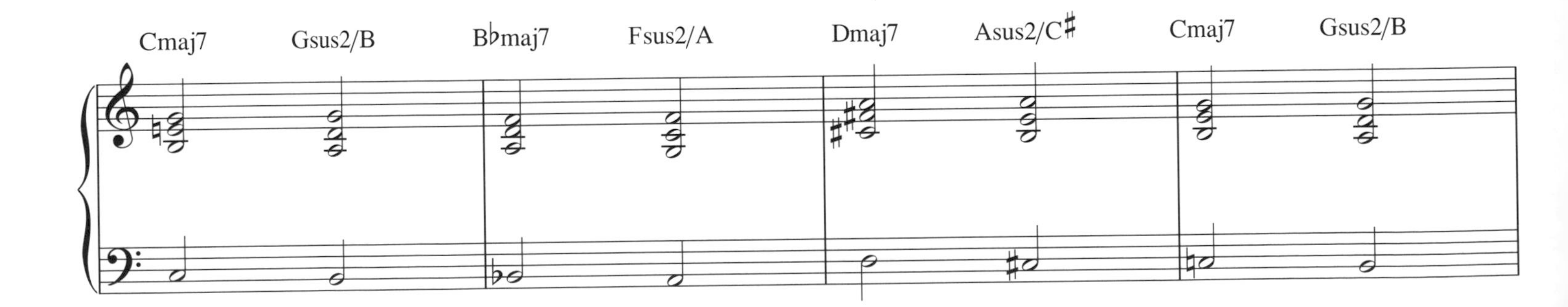
Cmaj7
Gsus2/B
B♭maj7
Fsus2/A
Dmaj7
Asus2/C♯
Cmaj7
Gsus2/B

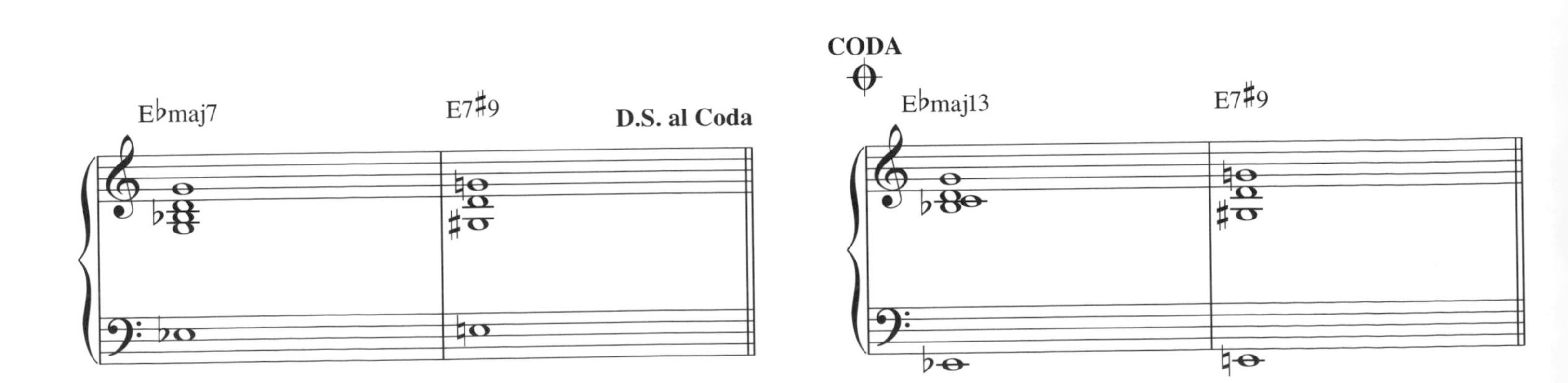
E♭maj7
E7♯9
D.S. al Coda
CODA
E♭maj13
E7♯9

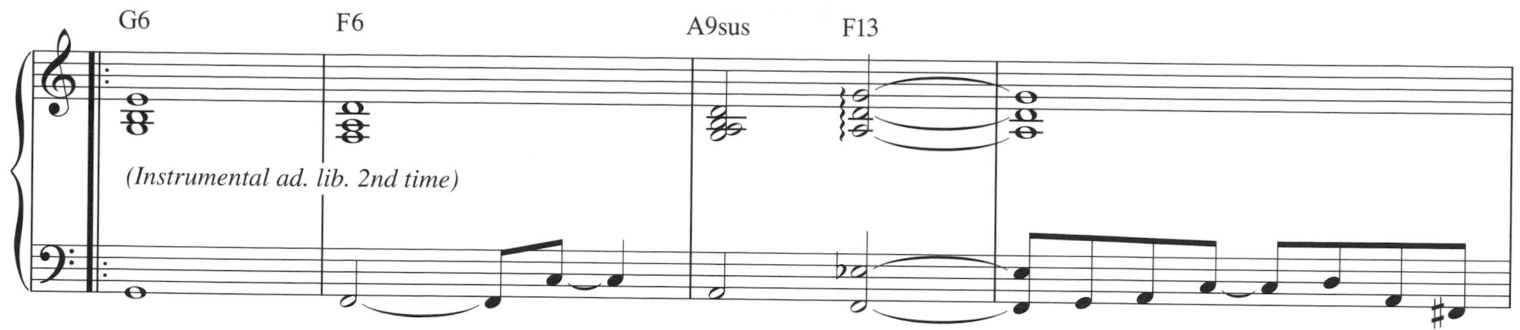
G6
F6
A9sus
F13
(Instrumental ad. lib. 2nd time)

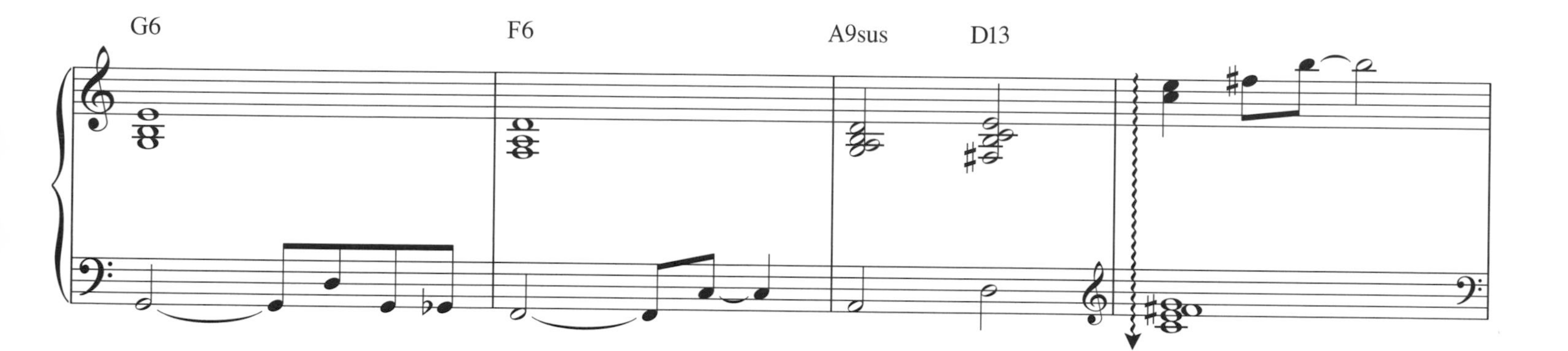
G6
F6
A9sus
D13

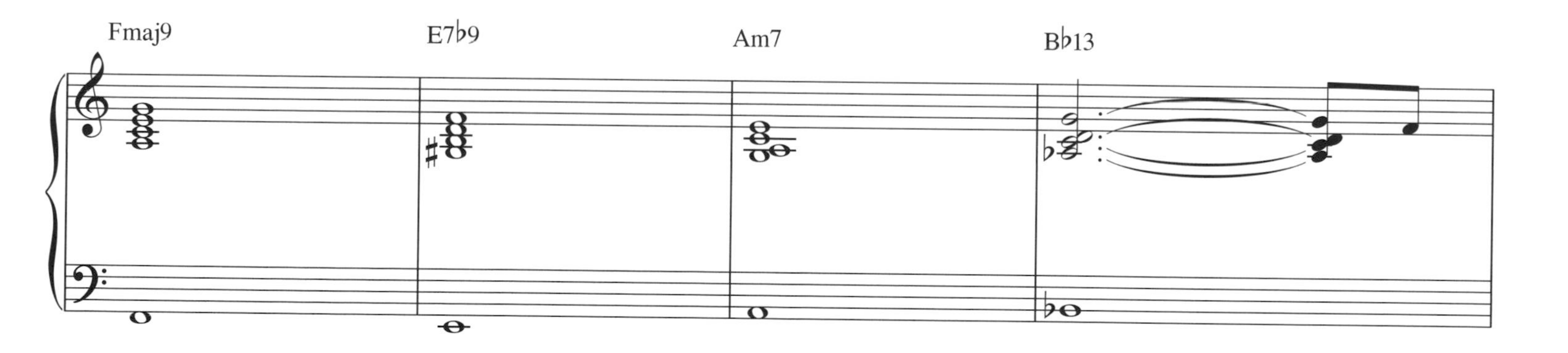
Fmaj9
E7♭9
Am7
B♭13

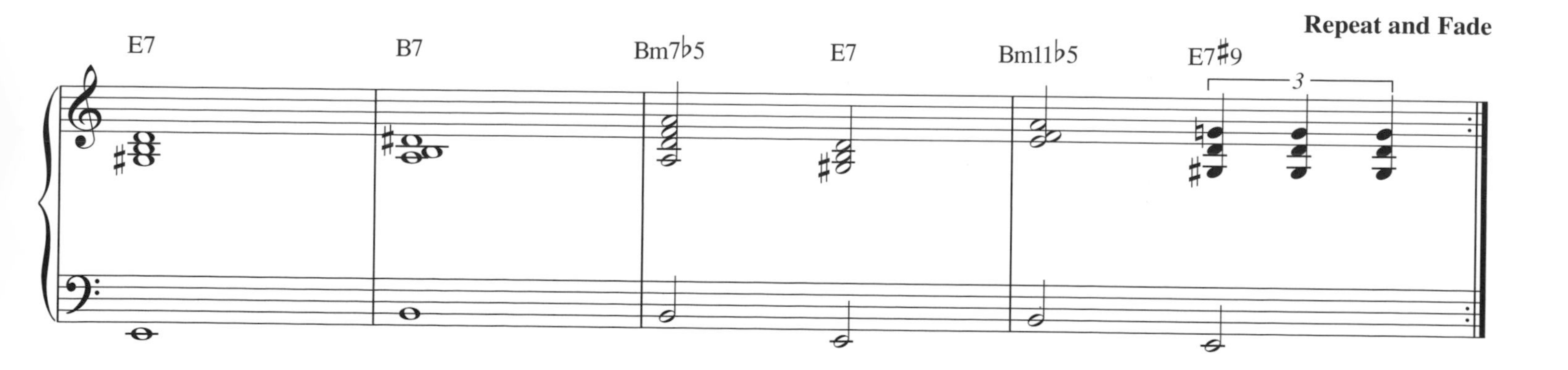
Repeat and Fade
E7
B7
Bm7♭5
E7
Bm11♭5
E7♯9
3

(Everything I Do)
I Do It for You

from the Motion Picture ROBIN HOOD: PRINCE OF THIEVES

Words and Music by Bryan Adams,
Robert John Lange and Michael Kamen

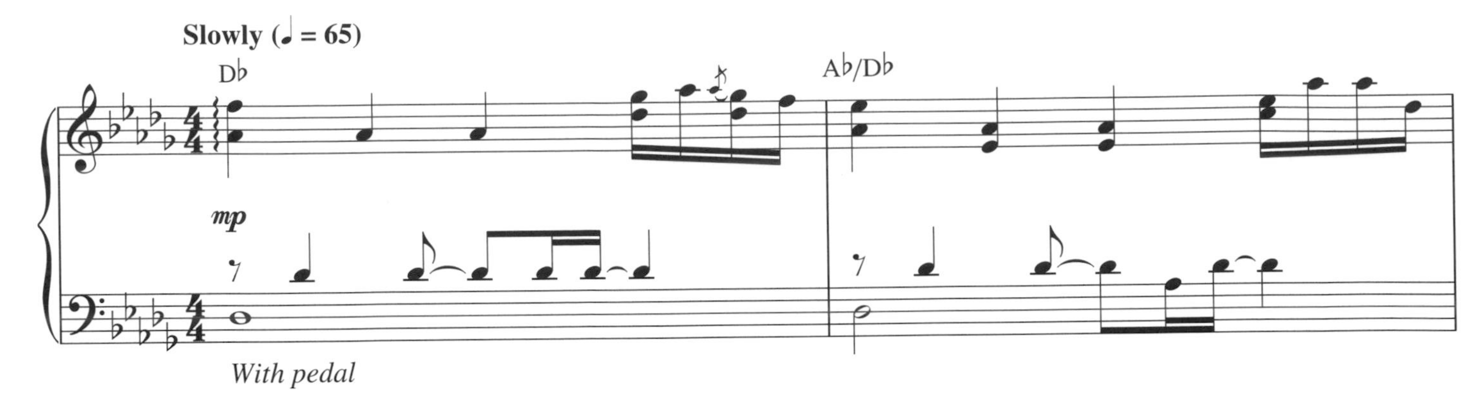

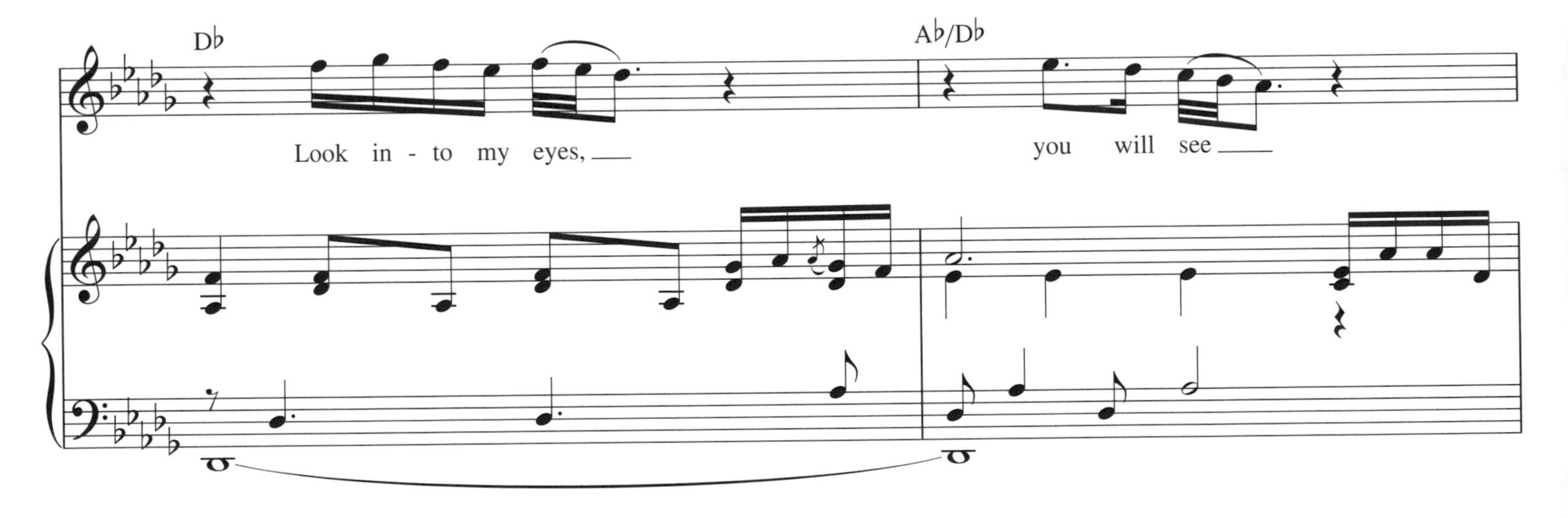

A♭/D♭
G♭/D♭
G♭
soul, and when you find me there you'll

D♭/A♭
A♭
E♭m
D♭/F
E♭m/G♭
D♭/F
search no more. Don't tell me it's not worth try - ing for. You can't

E♭m
D♭/F
E♭m/G♭
D♭/A♭
tell me it's not worth dy - ing for. You know it's true, ev - 'ry - thing I

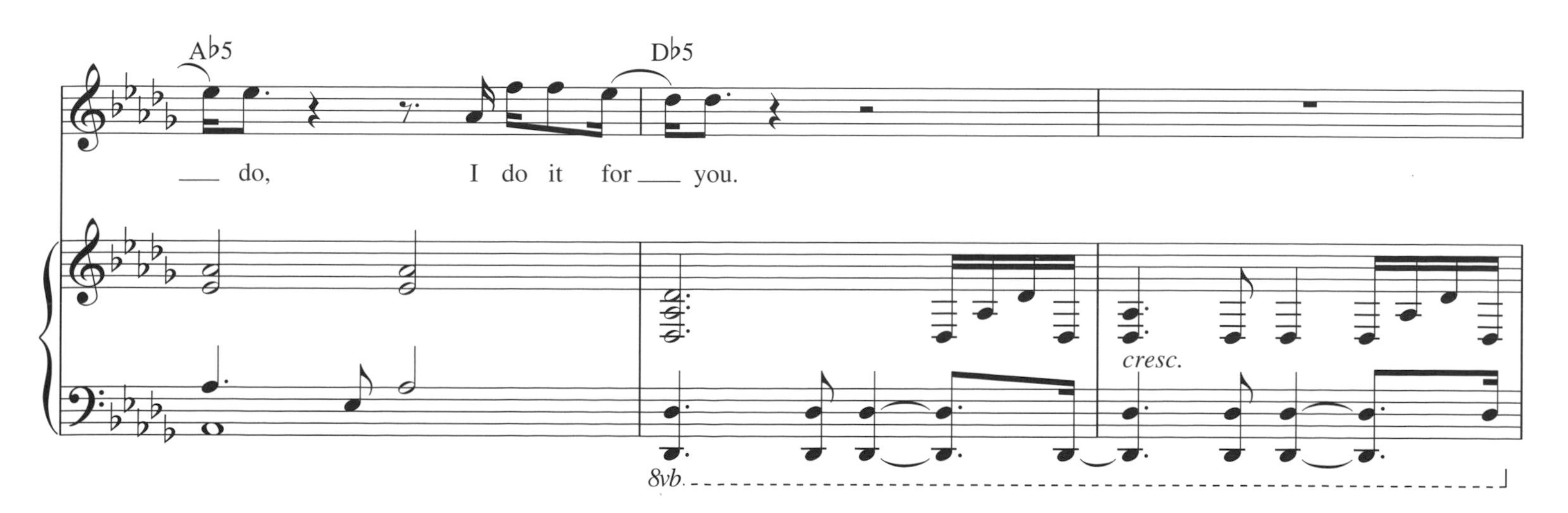
A♭5
D♭5
do, I do it for you.
cresc.
8vb.

D♭
A♭/D♭
Look in - to your heart, you will find there's
mf
G♭(add2)
A♭sus
D♭
noth - ing there to hide. Take me as I am, take my
A♭/D♭
G♭
D♭
A♭
life. I would give it all, I would sac - ri - fice. Don't
E♭m
D♭
E♭m
D♭/E♭
E♭m
D♭
tell me it's not worth fight - ing for. I can't help it, there's noth - ing I want

E♭m
D♭
more. You know it's true, ev - 'ry - thing I

A♭5
D♭5
D♭
do, I do it for you. Oh, yeah. There's
8vb

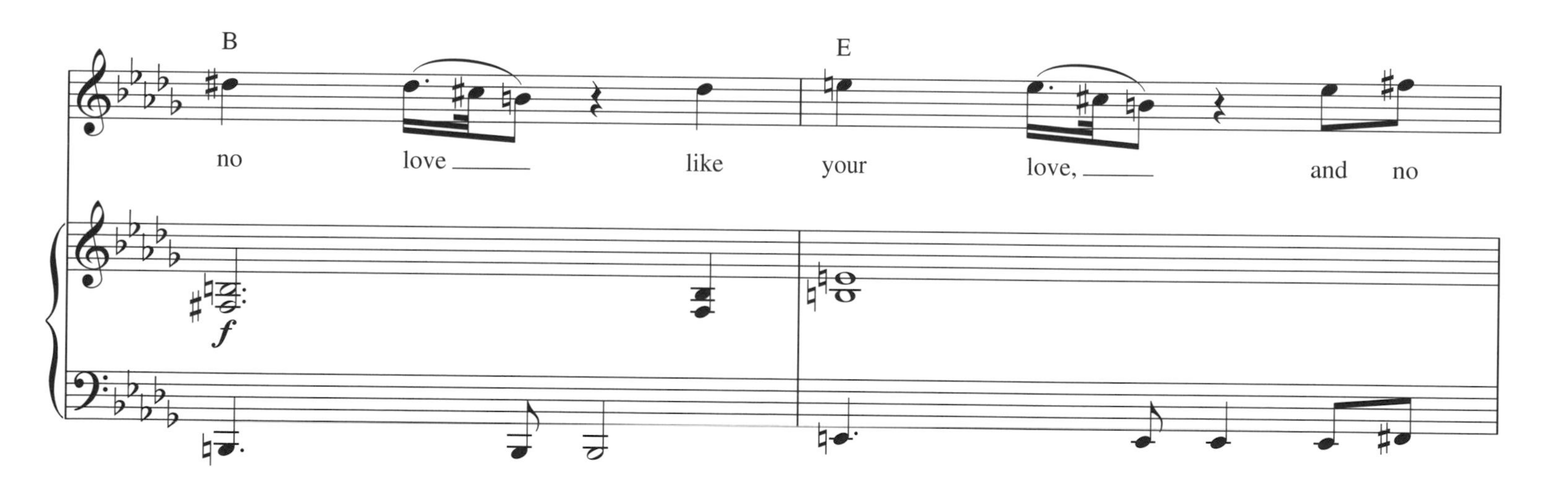
B
E
no love like your love, and no

B
F♯
oth - er could give more love. There's

D♭
A♭
no - where ___ un - less you're ___ there all the

E♭
A♭5
A♭sus
A♭5
N.C.
time, ___ all the way, _ yeah. ___
mf

G♭
A♭7
D♭

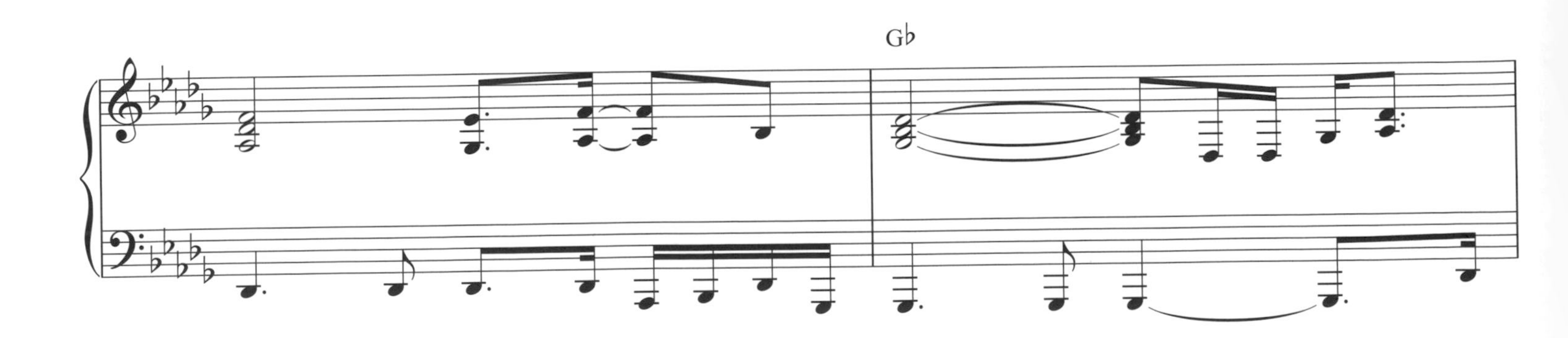

G♭

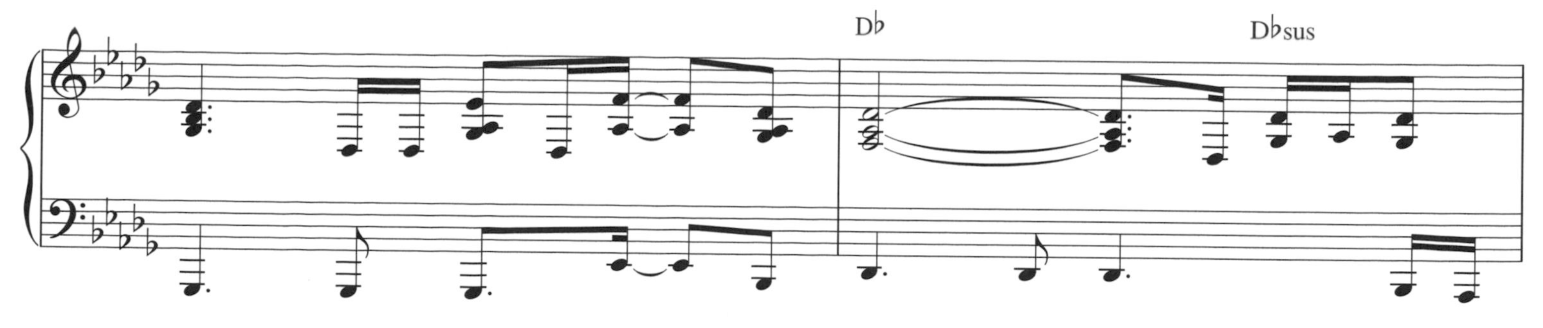
D♭
D♭sus

D♭
E♭m
Oh, you can't tell me it's not worth try - ing
f

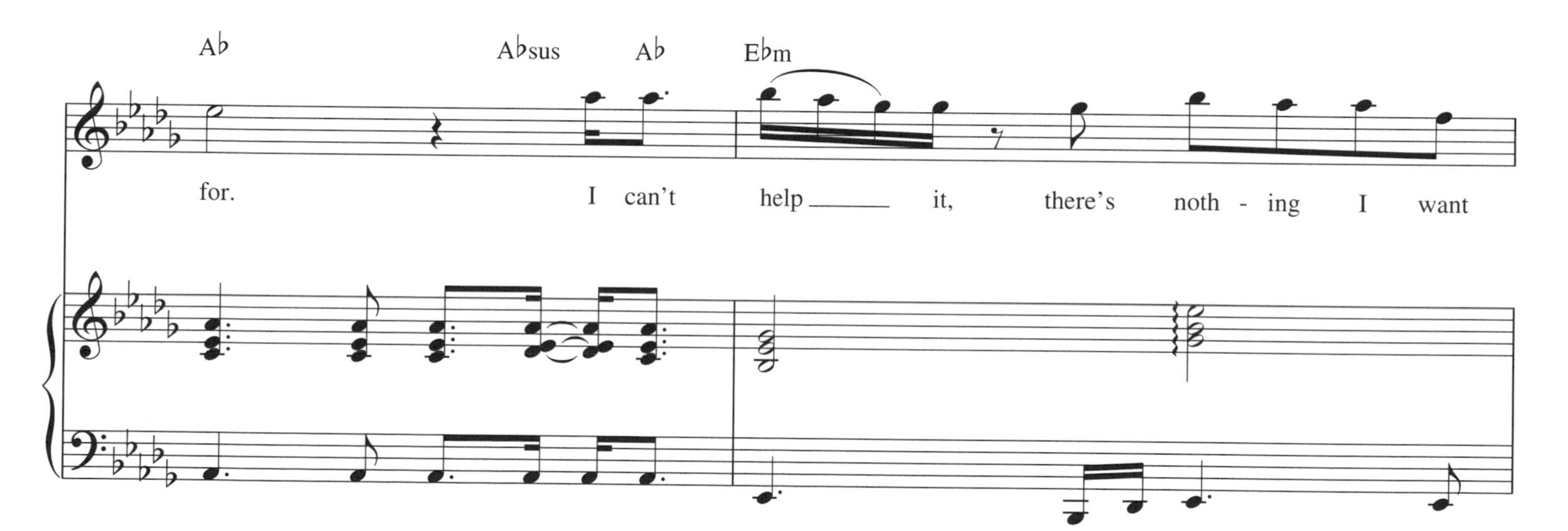
A♭
A♭sus
A♭
E♭m
for. I can't help it, there's noth - ing I want

A♭
A♭sus
A♭
D♭
more. Yeah, I would fight for you, I'd

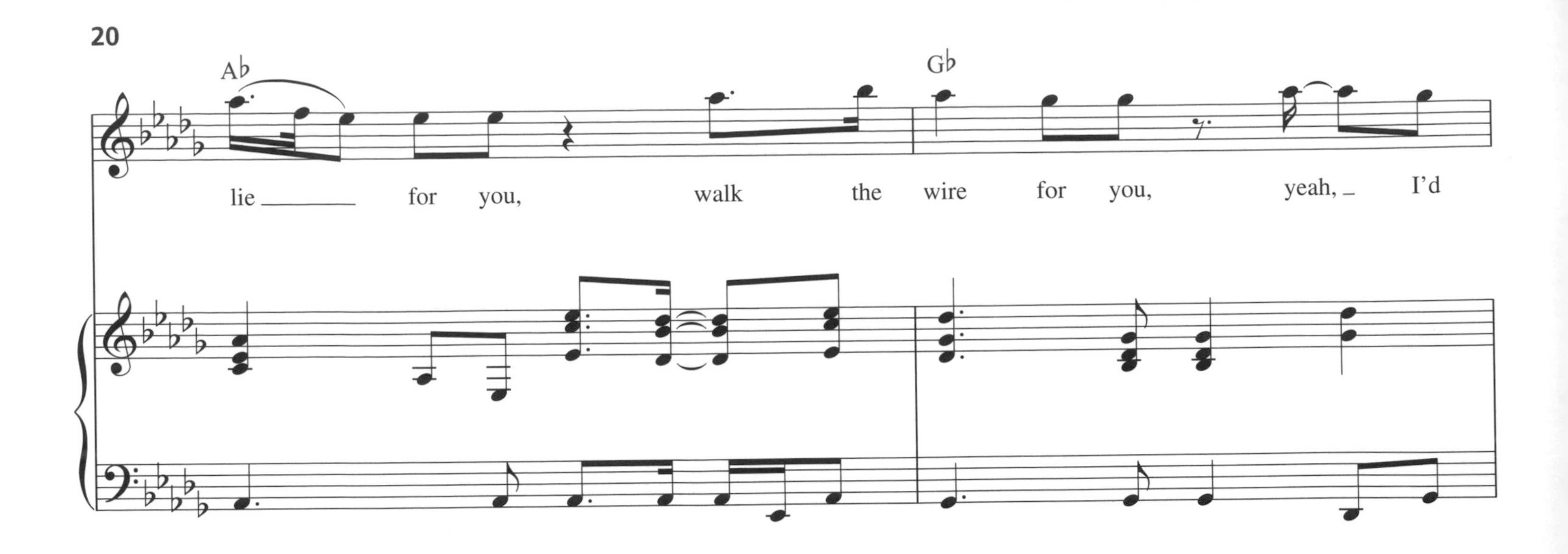
A♭
G♭
lie for you, walk the wire for you, yeah, I'd

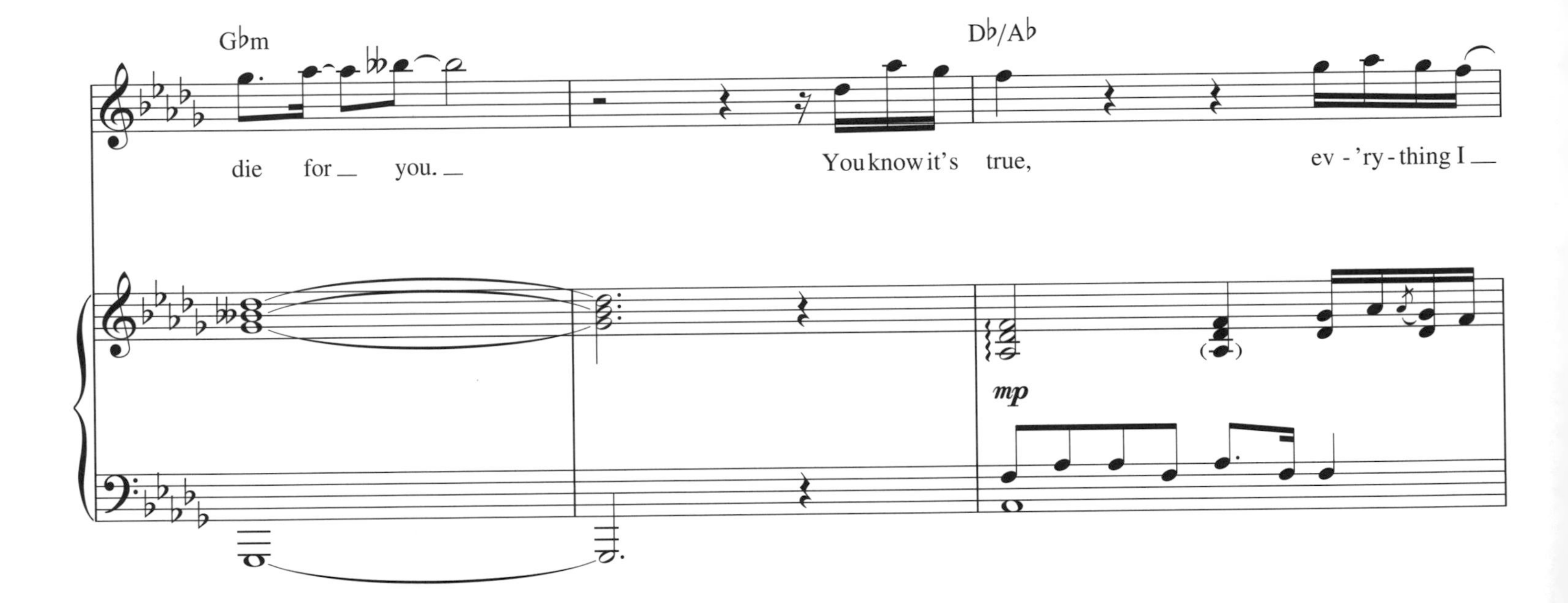
G♭m
D♭/A♭
die for you. You know it's true, ev - 'ry - thing I
mp

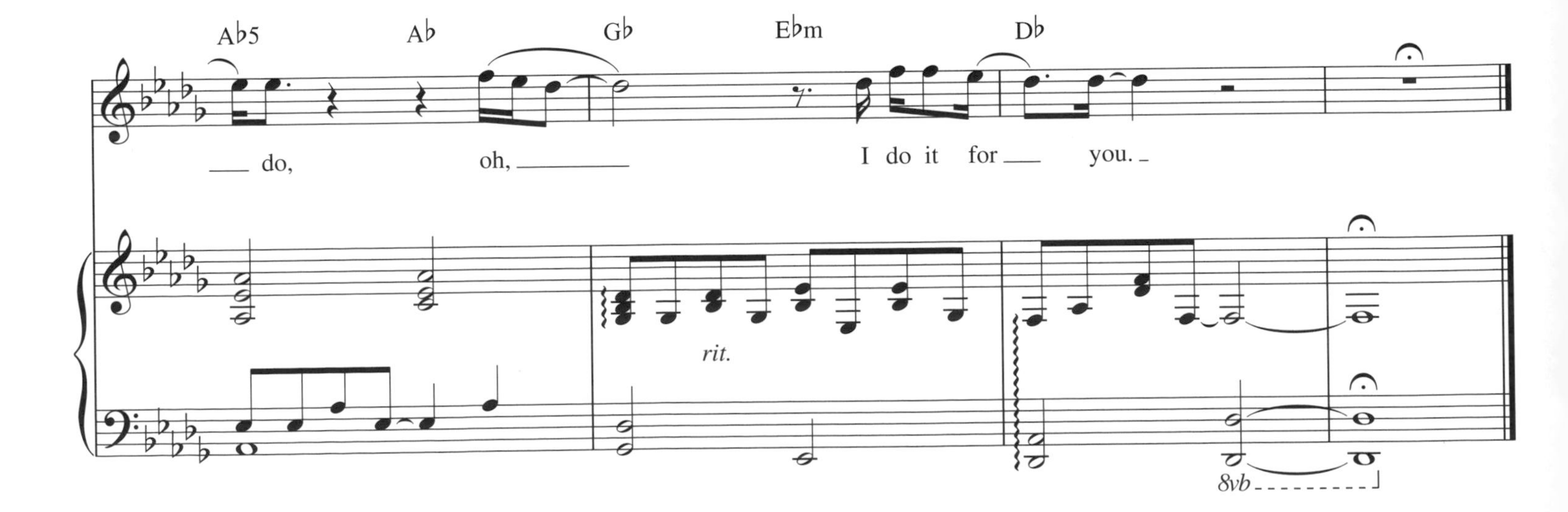
A♭5
A♭
G♭
E♭m
D♭
do, oh, I do it for you.
rit.
8vb

Hard to Say I'm Sorry

Words and Music by Peter Cetera
and David Foster

Slow Ballad (♩ = 71)
E
A/C♯
B/D♯
B/C♯
G♯/B♯
mf
3

C♯m
C♯m/B
F♯/A♯
Bsus
B
E

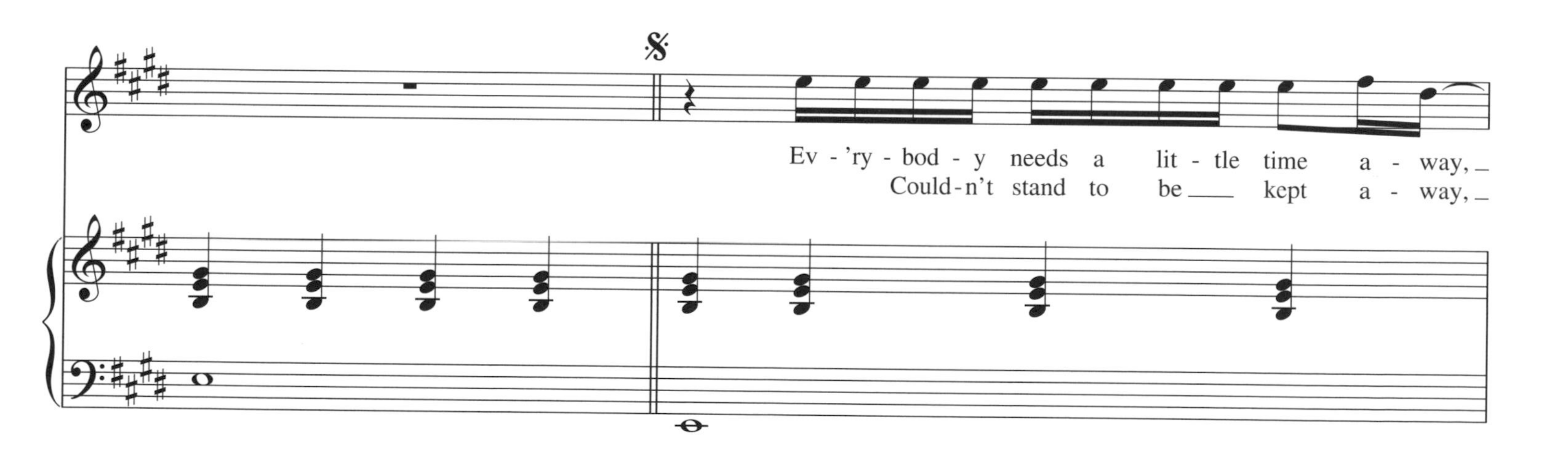
Ev - 'ry - bod - y needs a lit - tle time a - way,
Could - n't stand to be kept a - way,

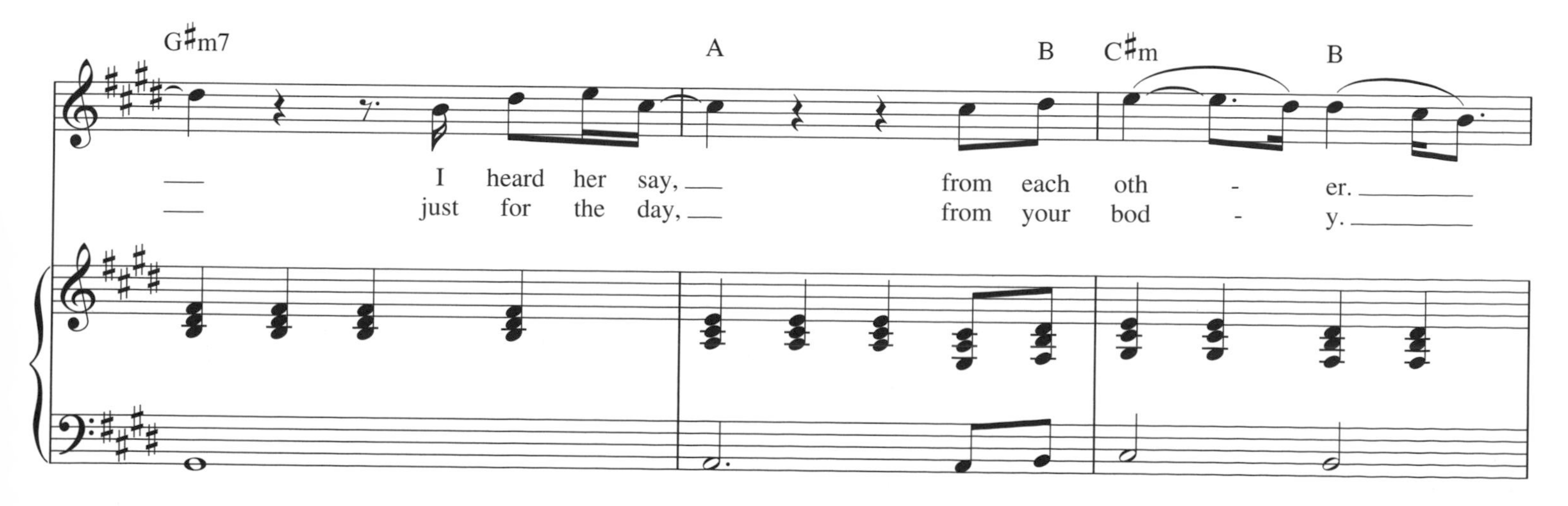
G♯m7
A
B
C♯m
B
I heard her say, from each oth - er.
just for the day, from your bod - y.

E
G♯m7
A
B
E - ven lov - ers need a hol - i - day
Would - n't wan - na be swept a - way
far a - way from each
far a - way from the
C♯m
B
C♯m
F♯m7
E/B
B7
E
oth - er.
one that I love.
Hold me now, it's hard for me to say I'm sor - ry.
To Coda
C♯m
F♯m7
B7sus
B7
E
A/C♯
I just want you to stay.
know.
Af - ter all that we've been
B/D♯
B/C♯
G♯/B♯
C♯m
C♯m/B
F♯/A♯
E/B
B
B/C♯
B/D♯
through, I will make it up to you, I prom - ise to.

E
A/C♯
B/D♯
B/C♯
G♯7/B♯
And af - ter all that's been said and done, you're just
C♯m
C♯m/B
F♯7/A♯
Bsus
B
Bsus
B
D.S. al Coda
the part of me I can't let go.
Ooh.
CODA
C♯m
F♯m7
E/B
B7
A/E
E
E/D♯
Hold me now, I real - ly wan - na tell you I'm sor - ry.
C♯m7
F♯m7
B7sus
B7
E
A/C♯
I could nev - er let you go.
Af - ter all that we've been
rit.
a tempo
8vb

B/D♯ B/C♯ G♯/B♯ C♯m C♯m/B F♯/A♯ E/B B B/C♯ B/D♯
through, I will make it up to you, I prom - ise to.
E A/C♯ B/D♯ B/C♯ G♯7/B♯
And af - ter all that's been said and done, you're just
C♯m C♯m/B F♯/A♯ B B/A
the part of me I can't let go.
G C/E D/F♯ D/E B/D♯ Em Em/D A/C♯
Af - ter all that we've been through I will make it up to you, I prom-

D
Em7
D/F♯
G
C/E
D
D/E
B/D♯
- ise to.

Em
Em/D
A/C♯
D
Em7
D/F♯
G
C/E

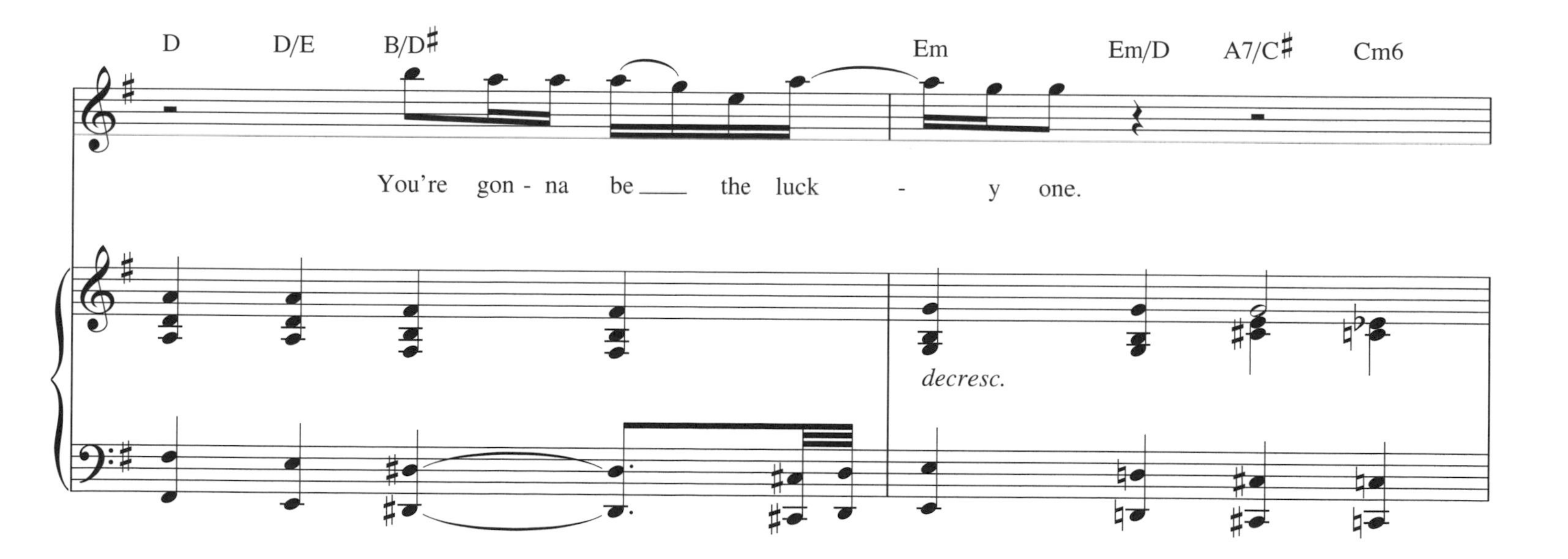
D
D/E
B/D♯
Em
Em/D
A7/C♯
Cm6
You're gon - na be the luck - y one.
decresc.

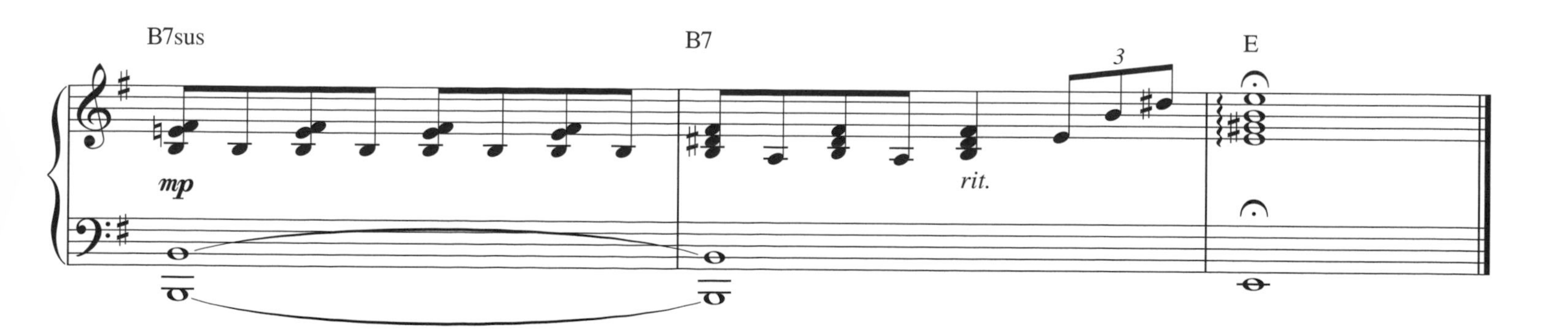
B7sus
B7
E
3
mp
rit.

Kiss on My List

Words and Music by Janna Allen
and Daryl Hall

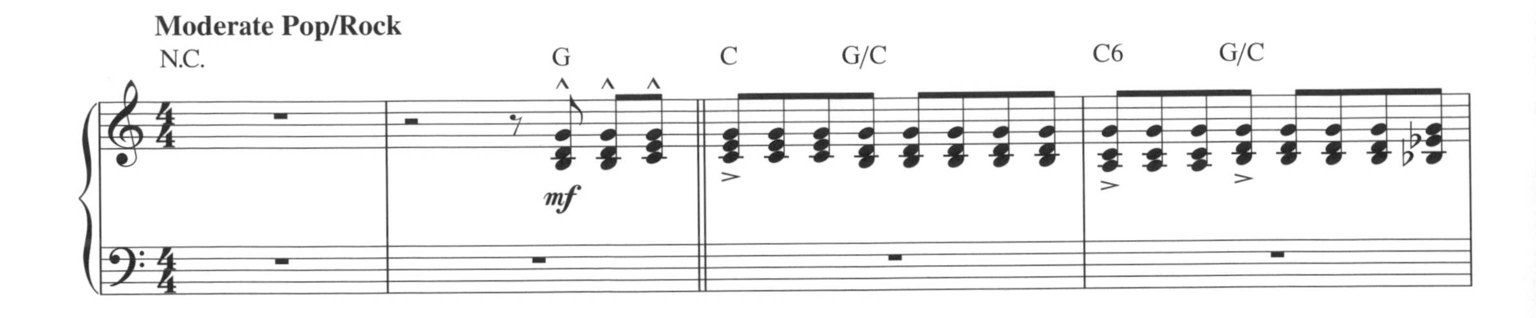

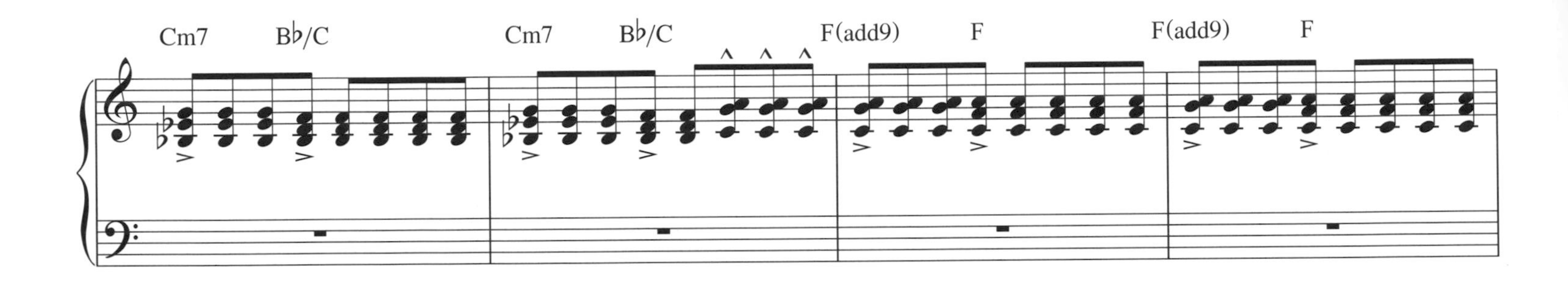

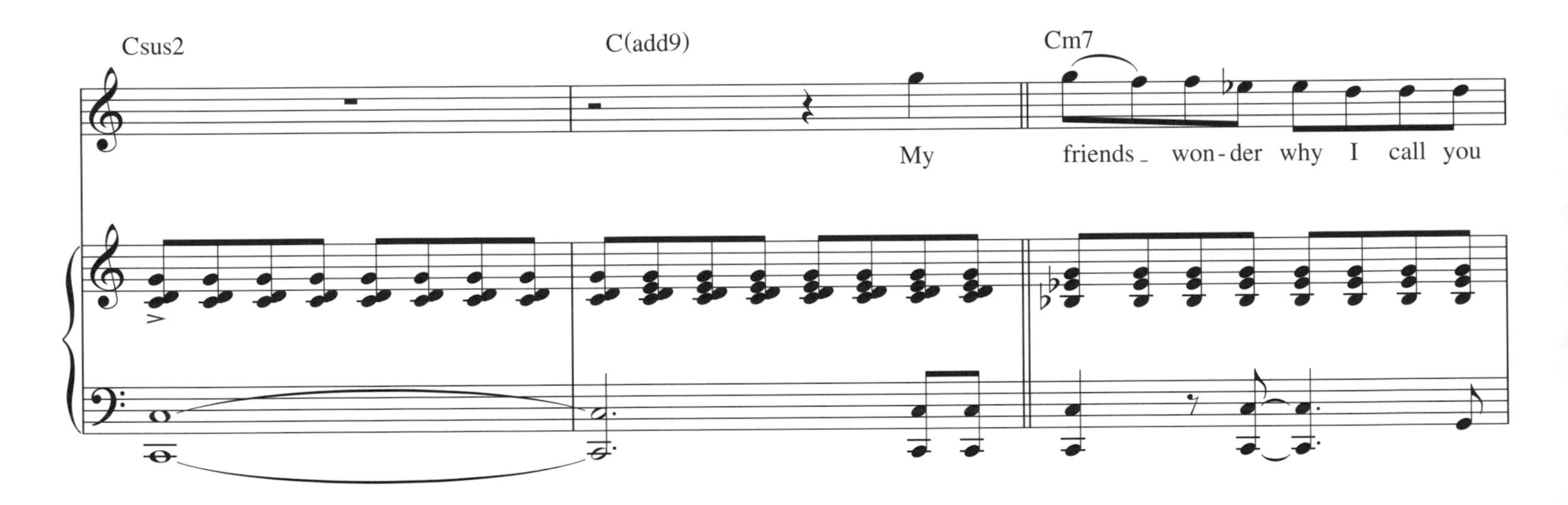

A♭
B♭9sus
B♭13sus
B♭9sus
Csus2
I don't feel the need to give such se - crets a - way.
C(add9)
Cm7
You think may - be I need help?
No, I know I'm right,
Fm9
Fm7
A♭6
al - right.
I'm just bet - ter off not
B♭9sus
B♭13sus
B♭9sus
C(add9)
lis - ten - ing to friends' ad - vice.
When they in -

Fm9
Dm11
Fm9
sist on know-ing my bliss, I tell them this,
sist on know-ing my bliss, I'll tell you this,

Dm11
Fm9
Dm11
when they wan-na know what the rea - son is, I on - ly
if you wan-na know what the rea - son is, I'll on - ly

Fm9
F/G
G
C
G/C
smile when I lie, then I tell them why: Be-cause your kiss, your kiss is on
smile when I lie, then I'll tell you why: (D.S.) kiss, your kiss is on
(No repeat on D.S.)

C6
G/C
Cm7
B♭/C
Cm7
my list, be-cause your kiss, your kiss is on my list, be-cause your
my list, be-cause your kiss, your kiss I can't re - sist, be-cause your

F(add9)
F
F(add9)
F
To Coda
1
G/C
C
G/C
kiss is on my list of the best things in life.
kiss is what I miss when I turn out the light.
C/G G7
2
Csus2
Be-cause your
I'd go
Cm7
Fm9
cra - zy won-der - in' what there is to real - ly see.
Fm7
A♭6
B♭9sus
B♭13sus
B♭9sus
3
Let the night just take up your time, 'cause it means more to

Csus2
C(add9)
Cm7
me.
Some - times I for - get what I'm do -
Fm9
Fm7
ing, I don't for - get what I want,
what I want.
Re -
A♭6
B♭9sus
B♭13sus
B♭9sus
gret what I've done, re - gret you? I could-n't go on.
C(add9)
D.S. al Coda
(Take 2nd verse)
But if you in -
CODA
Csus2
G/C
Instrumental solo
miss you, girl.)

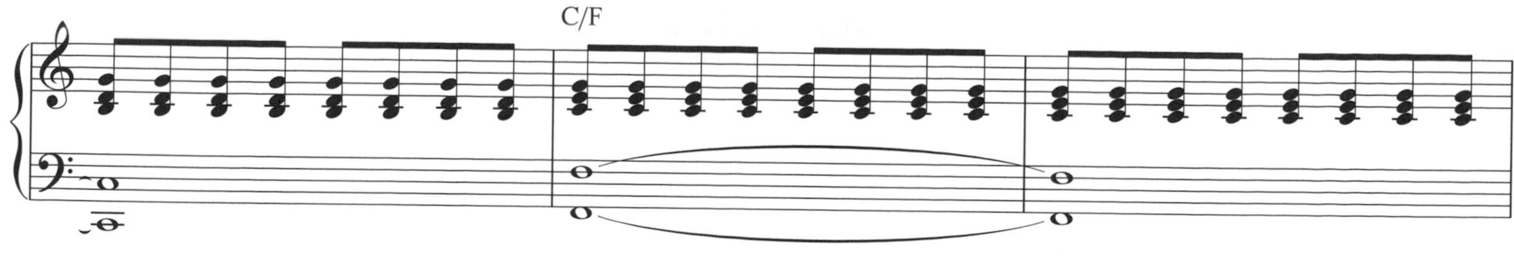
C/F

F/E♭
1
Dm7

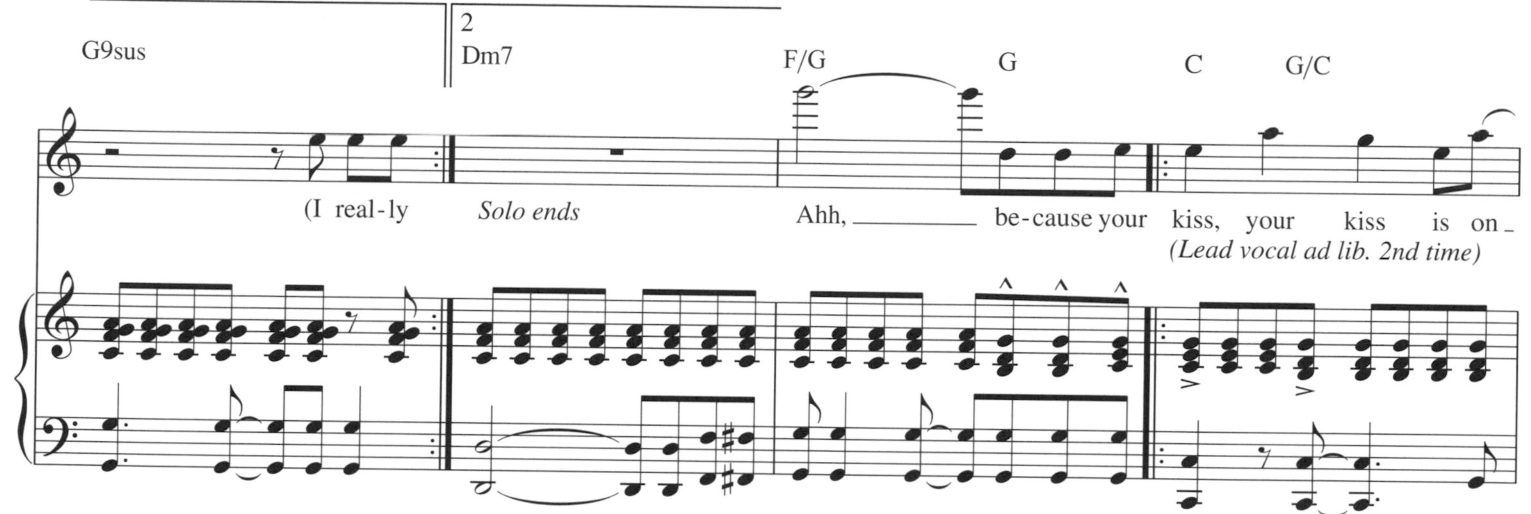
G9sus
2
Dm7
F/G
G
C
G/C
(I real-ly
Solo ends
Ahh, because your kiss, your kiss is on
(Lead vocal ad lib. 2nd time)

C6
C/G
Cm7
B♭/C
Cm7
my list, because your kiss, your kiss
is on my list,
I can't re-sist,
be-cause your

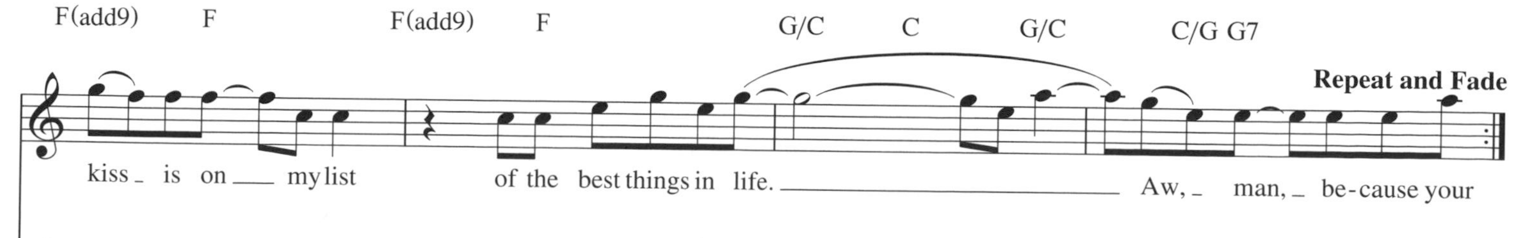
F(add9)
F
F(add9)
F
G/C
C
G/C
C/G G7
Repeat and Fade
kiss is on my list of the best things in life.
Aw, man, be-cause your

My Life

Words and Music by
Billy Joel

D9
C9
E♭maj7/F
F7
8vb
B♭
D
D(add9)/F♯
Got a call from an old friend, we used to be real
They will tell you you can't sleep a - lone in a strange
mf
8vb
G
close.
place,
A
Said he could - n't go on
then they'll tell you you can't
the A - mer - i - can way.
sleep with some - bod - y else.
D
G/D
D

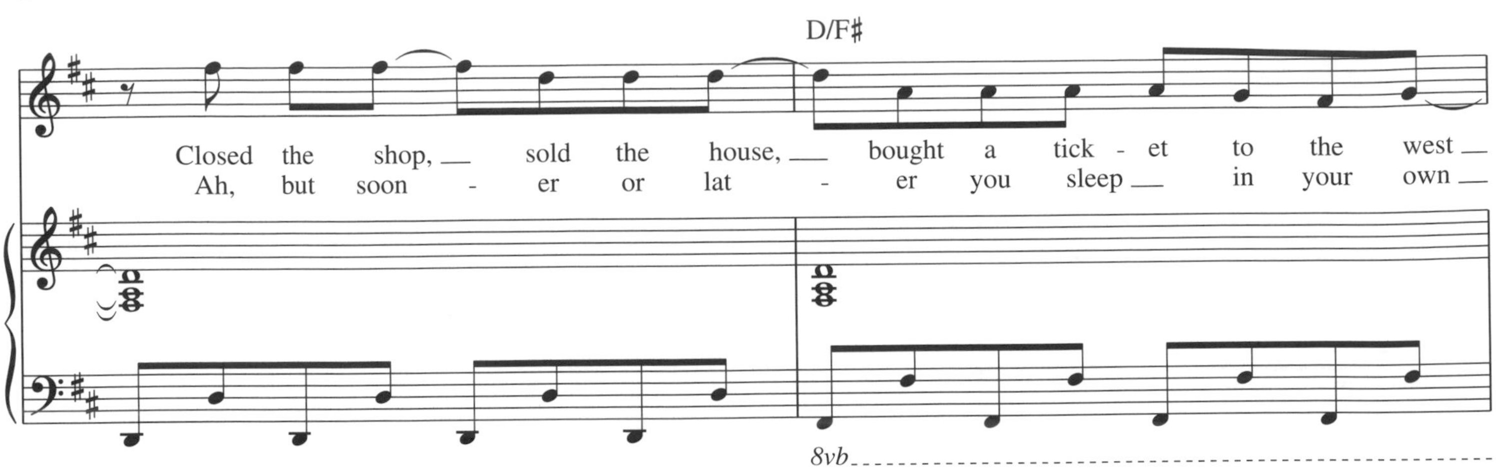
D/F♯
Closed the shop, sold the house, bought a tick - et to the west
Ah, but soon - er or lat - er you sleep in your own
8vb

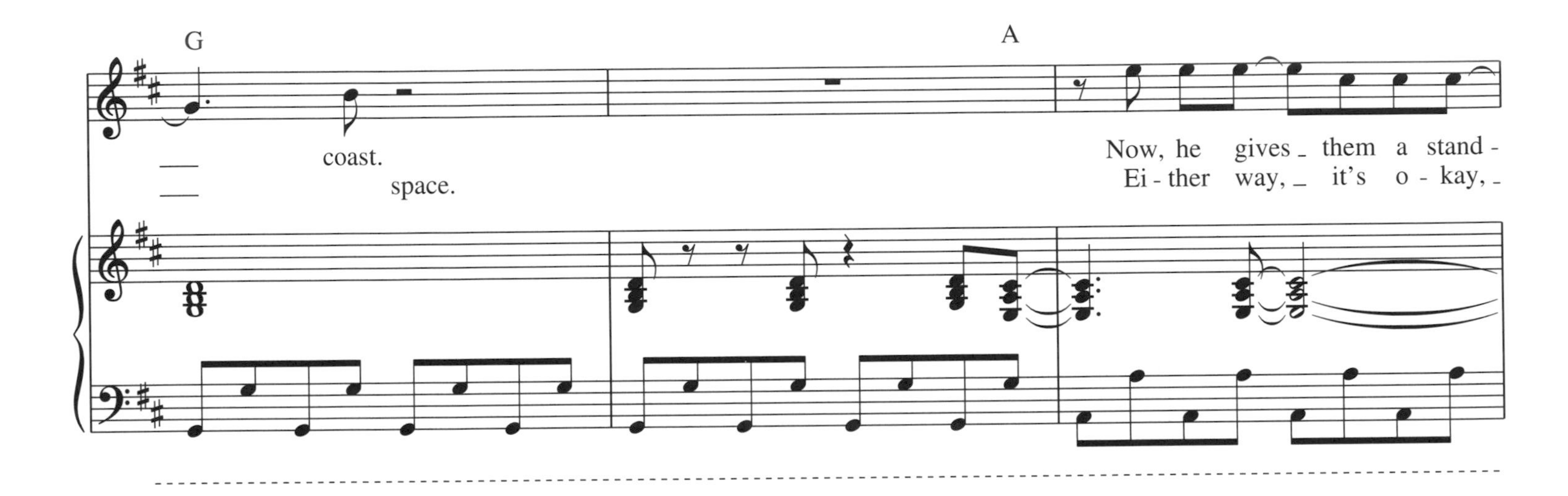
G
A
coast.
space.
Now, he gives them a stand -
Ei - ther way, it's o - kay,

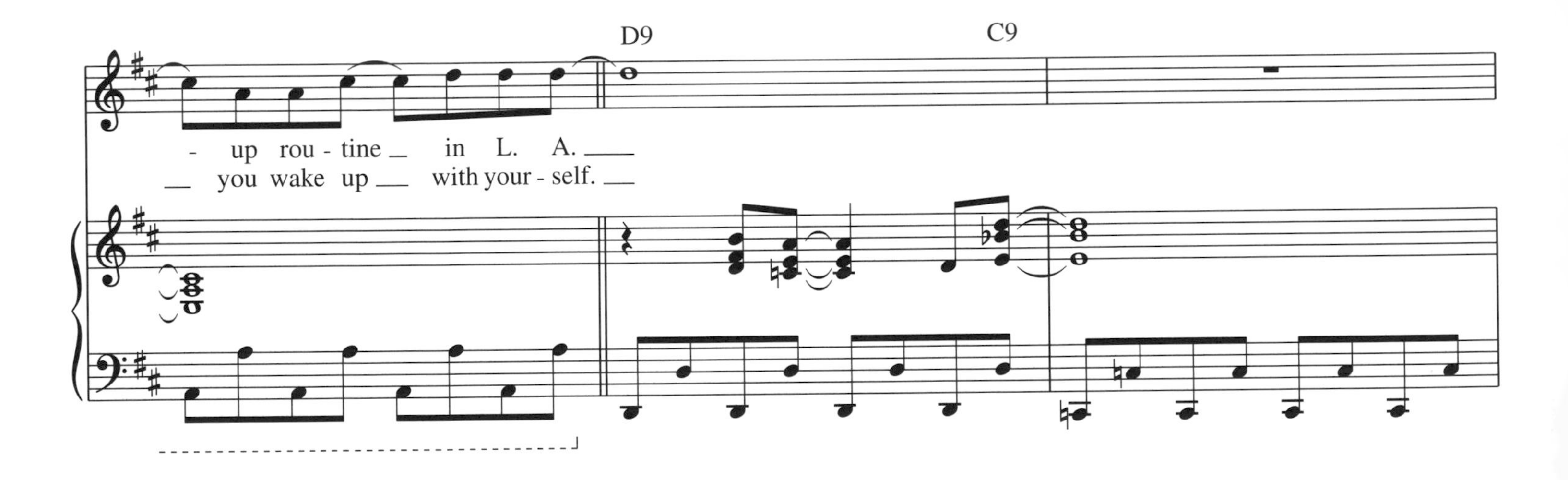
D9
C9
- up rou - tine in L. A.
you wake up with your - self.

E♭maj7/F
F7
B♭
D7
C9
8vb

E♭maj7/F
F7
B♭
To Coda
8vb
D
D/F♯
G
I don't need_ you to wor - ry for me_ 'cause I'm al - right.
8vb
A
I don't want_ you to tell_ me it's time_ to come home._
D
G/D
D
G/D
D
I don't care_ what you say_

D/F♯
G
D/F♯ Em7 D A
an - y - more, this is my life.
8vb
Go a - head with your own life. Leave me a - lone.
𝄋𝄋 Bridge
Bm
I nev - er
2nd time - sim.
said you had to of - fer me a sec - ond chance.
F♯7/C♯
mp
mf
mp
D7
I nev - er said I was a vic - tim of cir - cum - stance.
E9

N.C.
G
D/F#
I still be - long.
f
8vb

F#7
Bm
E7sus
Don't get me wrong.
And you can speak
8vb

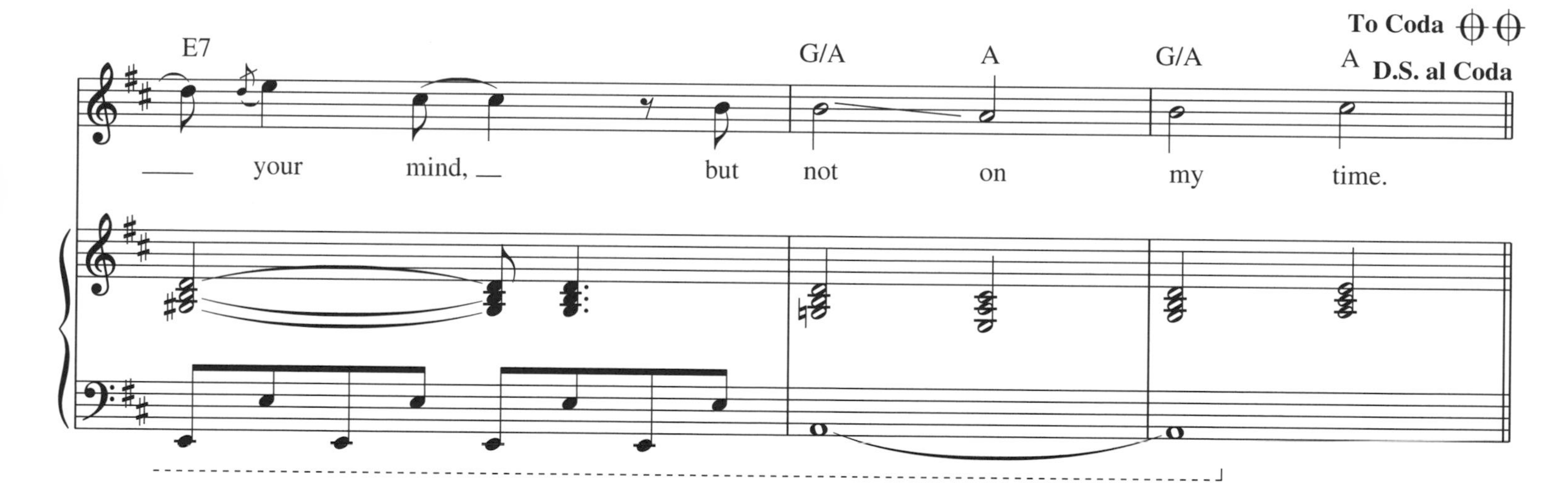
E7
G/A
A
G/A
A
To Coda
D.S. al Coda
your mind, but not on my time.

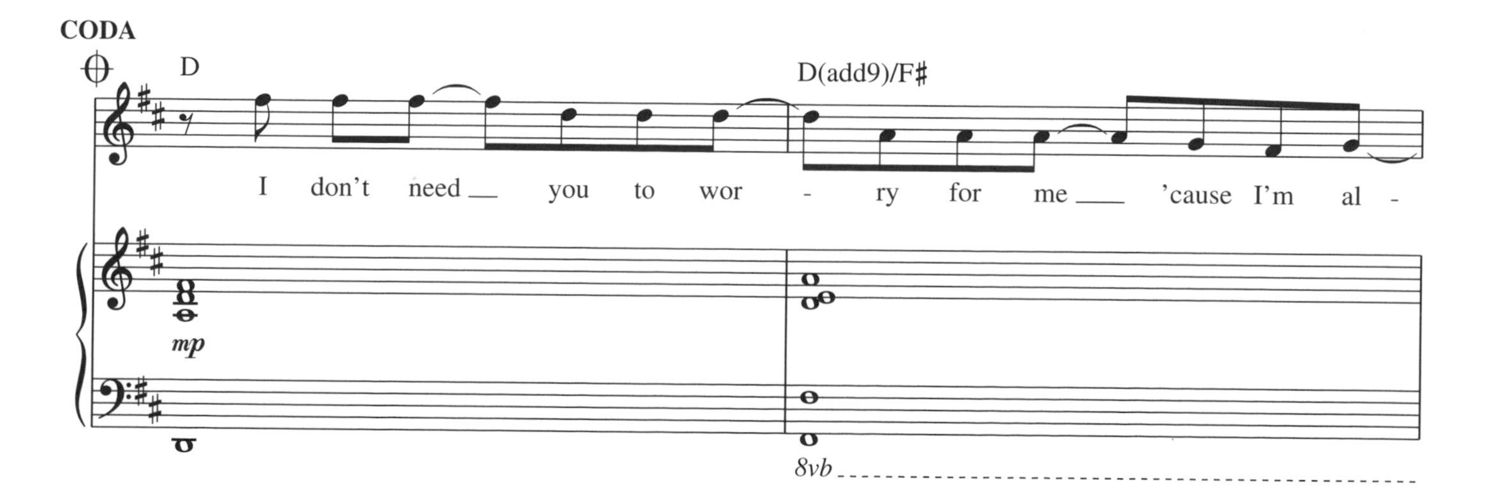
CODA
D
D(add9)/F#
I don't need you to wor - ry for me 'cause I'm al -
mp
8vb

G
A
right.
I don't want you to tell
me it's time to come home.
D
D(add9)/F♯
G
I don't care what you say any-more, this is my life.
mf
8vb
D/F♯
Em7 D
A
D.S.S. al Coda
Go a-head with your own life. Leave me a-lone.
8vb

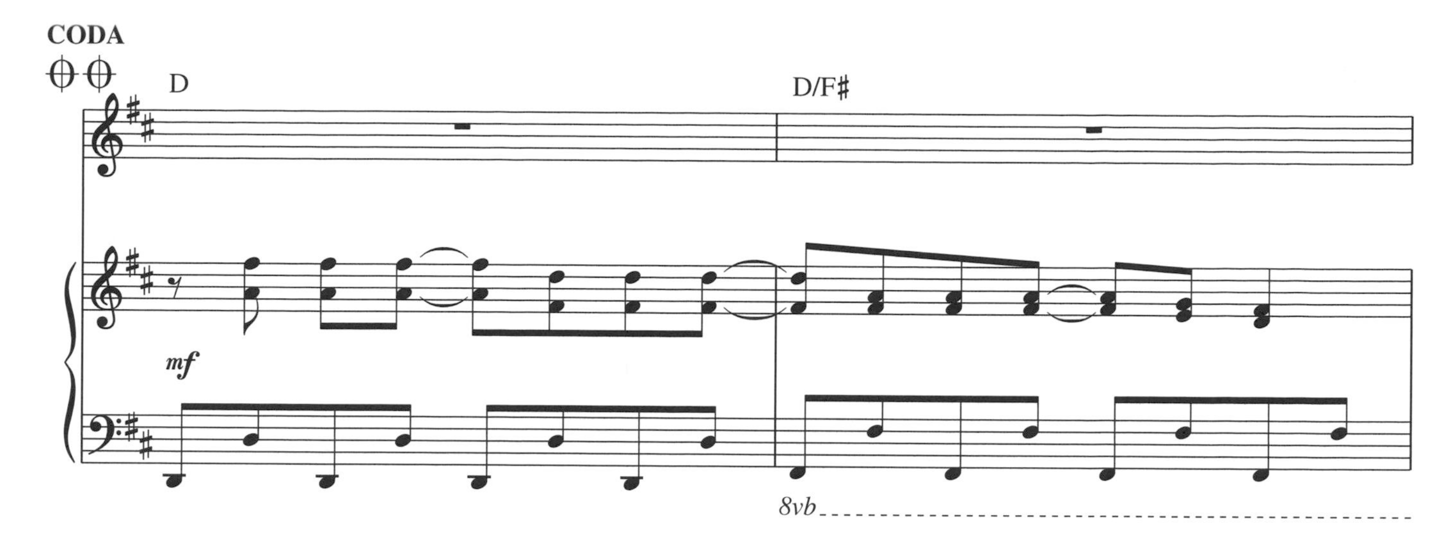
CODA
D
D/F#
mf
8vb

G
A

D
G/D
D G/D
Em7/D D

D/F#
I don't care what you say any - y - more, this is
8vb

G
D/F#
Em7 D
A
my life.
Go a - head with your own
life. Leave me a - lone.
(Begin Fade 2nd time)
D9
C9
Lead vocal 1st time only
Eb maj7/F
F7
Bb
D9
C9
(Keep it to your - self, it's my life.)
8vb
Eb maj7/F
F7
Bb
Repeat and Fade
(Keep it to your - self, it's my life.)
8vb

Walking in Memphis

Words and Music by
Marc Cohn

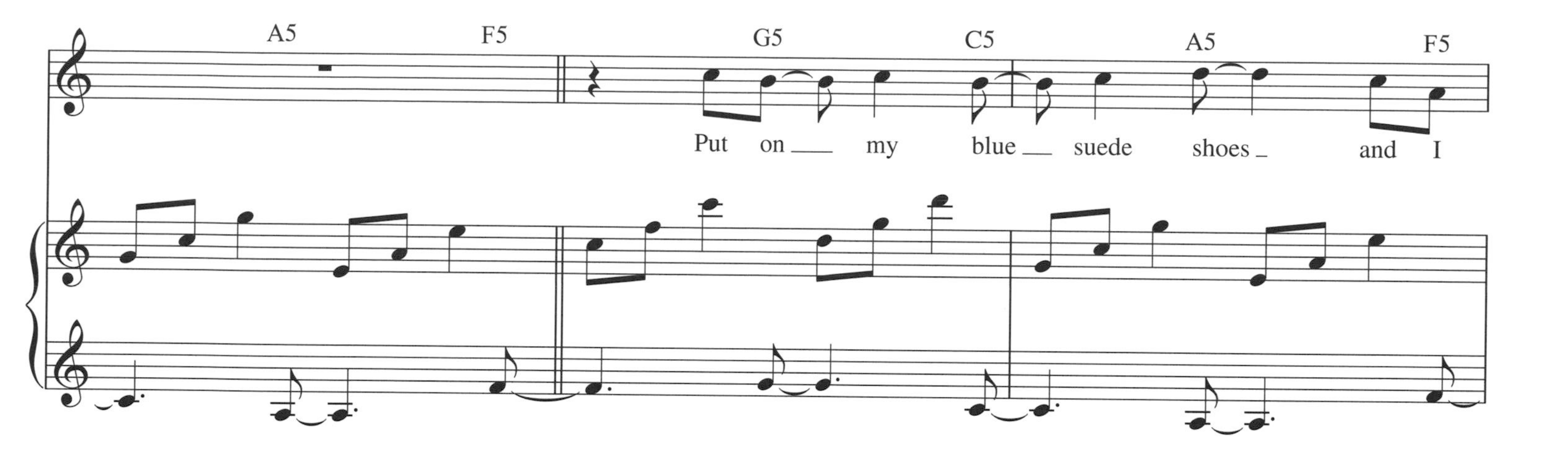

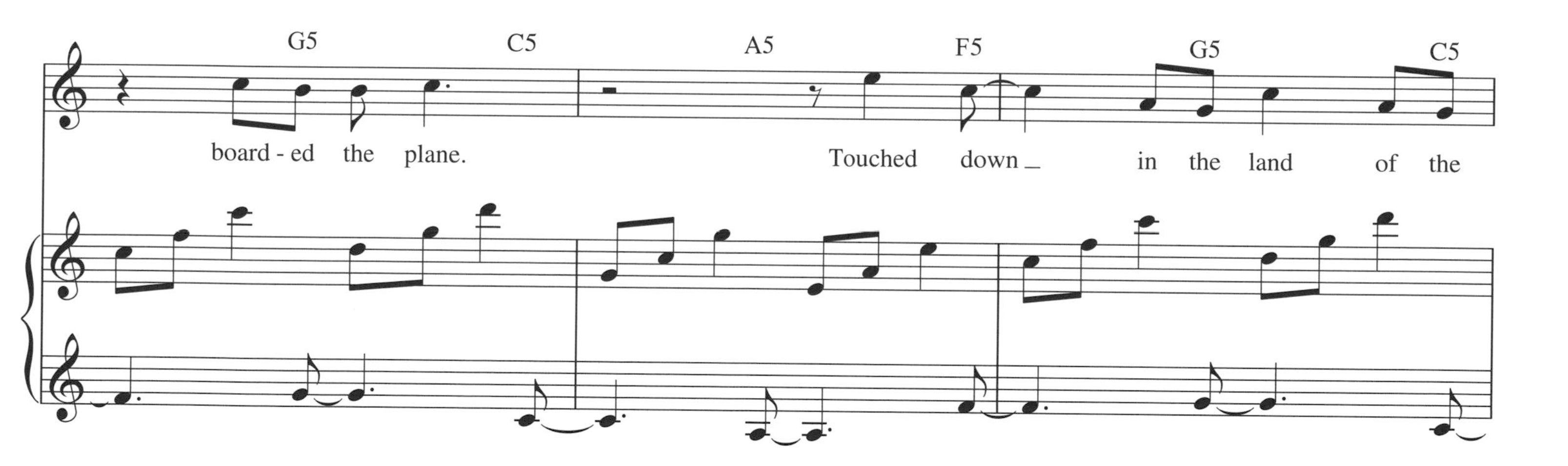

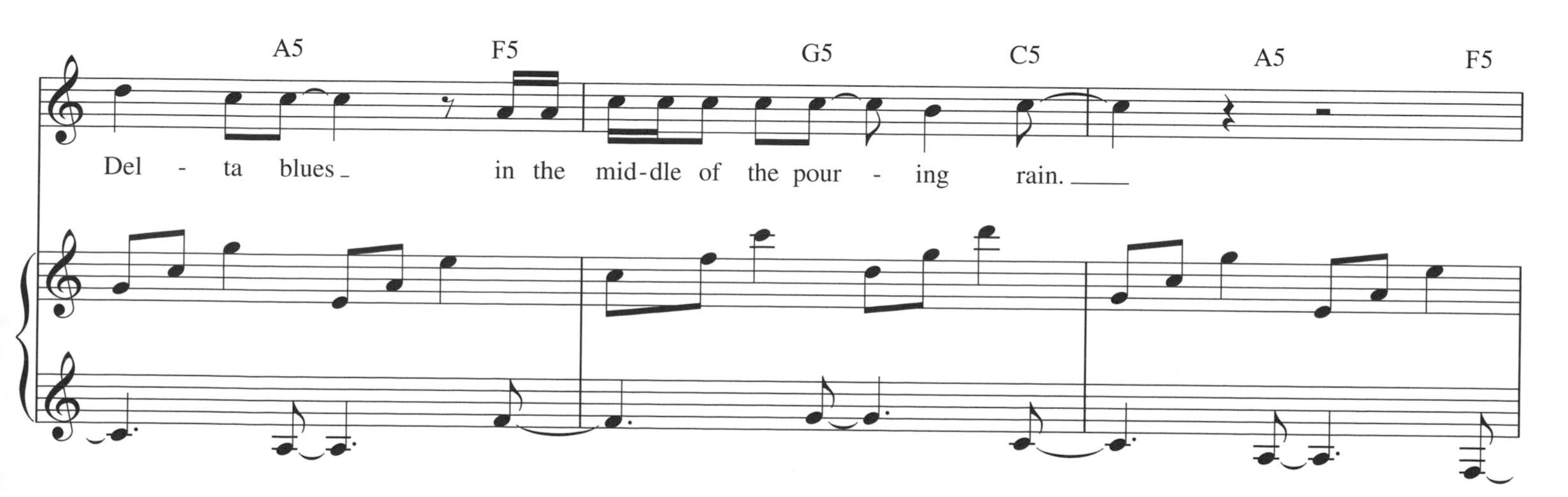

G5 C5 A5 F5 G5 C5
W. C. Han - dy, won't you look down o - ver me?
(dou - ble - u)
A5 F5 G5 C5 A5 F5
Yeah, I got a first - class tick - et, but I'm as
G5 C Am F G C
blue as a boy can be. Then I'm walk-ing in Mem - phis.
cresc.
mf
Am F G C Am
I was walk - ing with my feet ten feet off of Beale. Walk-ing in Mem-

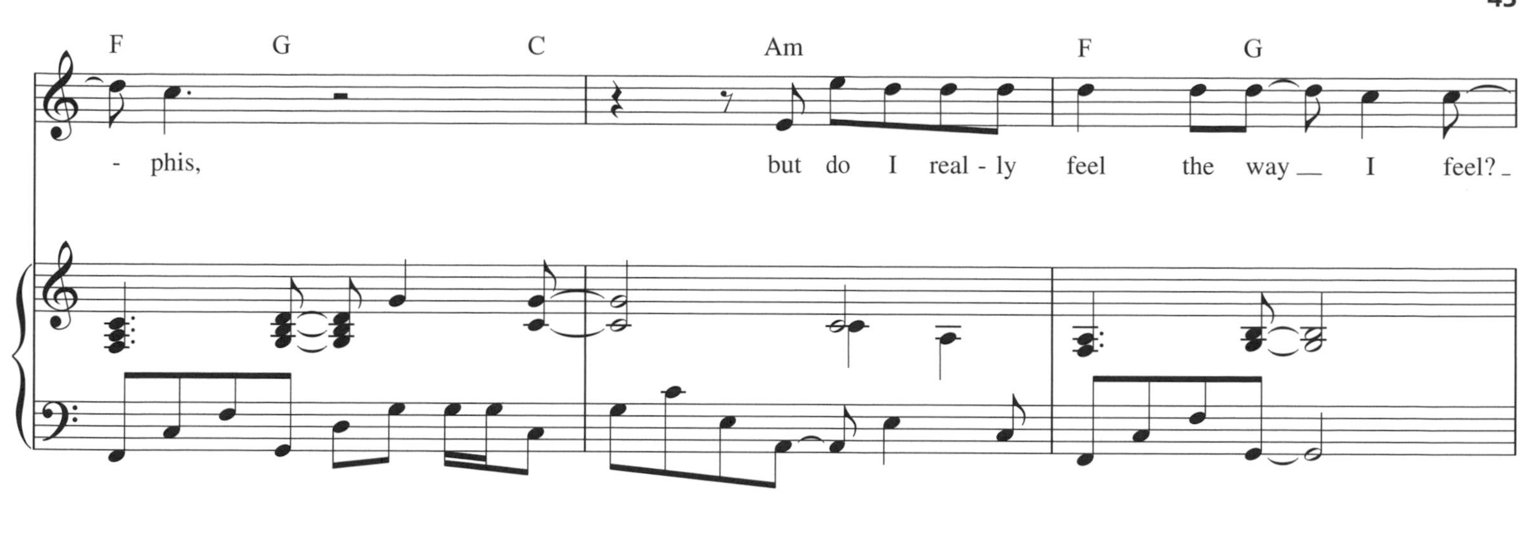
F G C Am F G
- phis, but do I real - ly feel the way I feel?

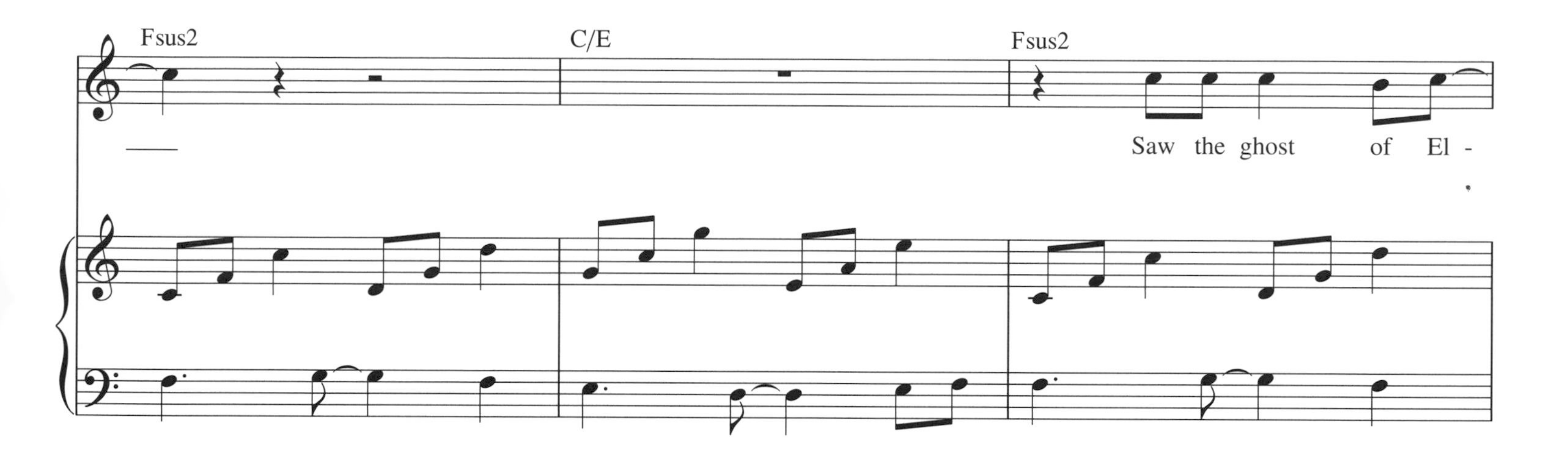
Fsus2 C/E Fsus2
Saw the ghost of El -

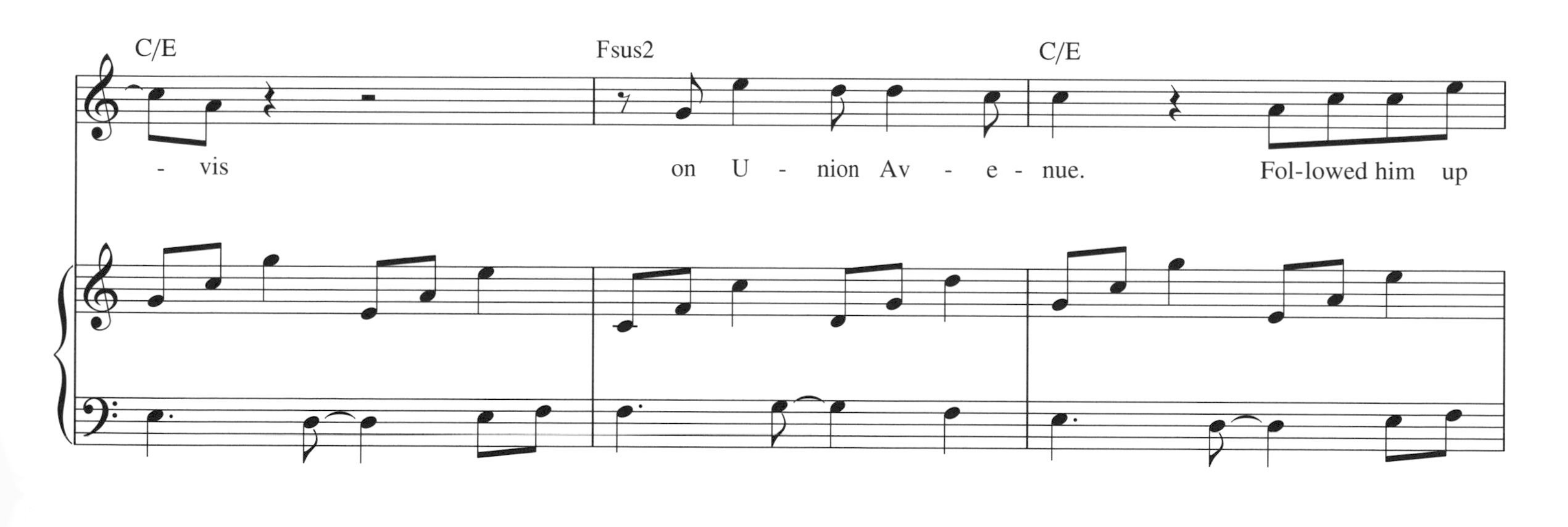
C/E Fsus2 C/E
- vis on U - nion Av - e - nue. Fol-lowed him up

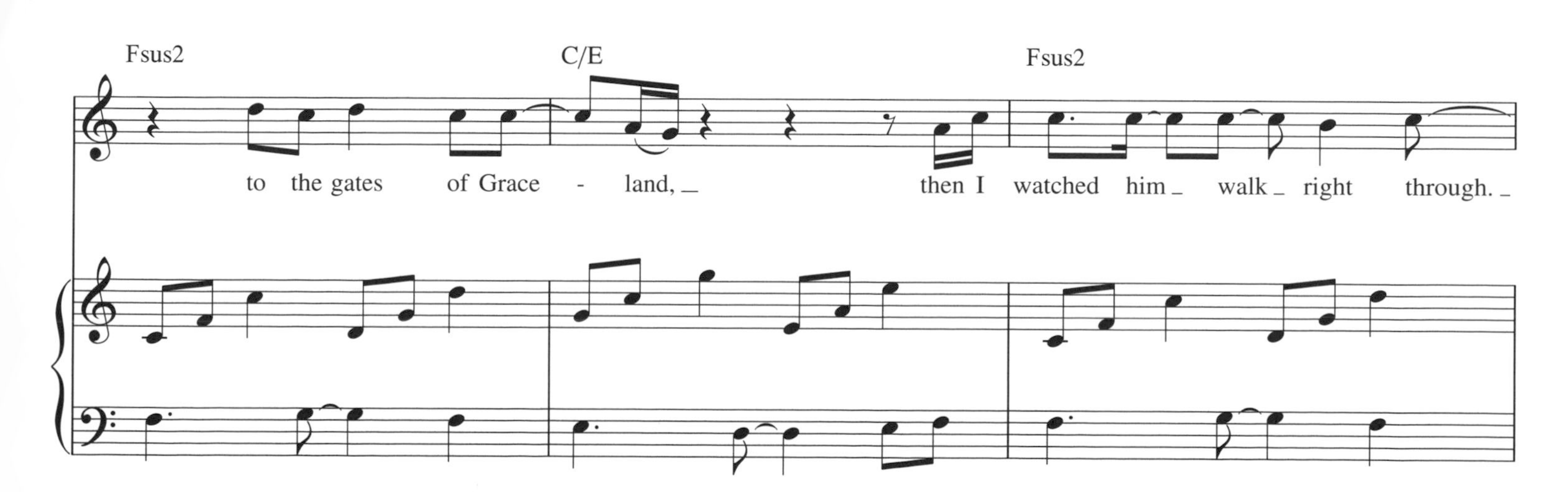
Fsus2 C/E Fsus2
to the gates of Grace - land, then I watched him walk right through.

C/E Fsus2 C
Now se - cu - ri - ty, they did not see him, they just
Fsus2 C Fsus2
hov - ered 'round his tomb, but there's a pret - ty lit - tle thing wait -
C Fmaj7 C
ing for the King down in the Jun - gle Room, when I was walk - ing in Mem -
F G C Am F G C
- phis. I was walk - ing with my feet ten feet off of Beale.

Am F G C Am
Walk-ing in Mem - phis, but do I real - ly

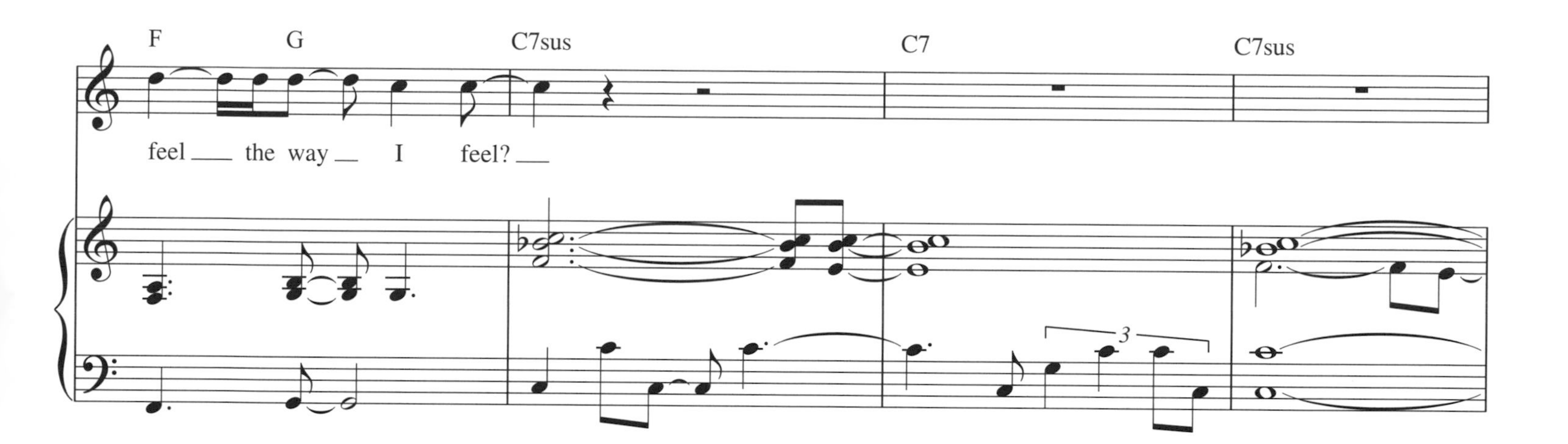
F G C7sus C7 C7sus
feel the way I feel?

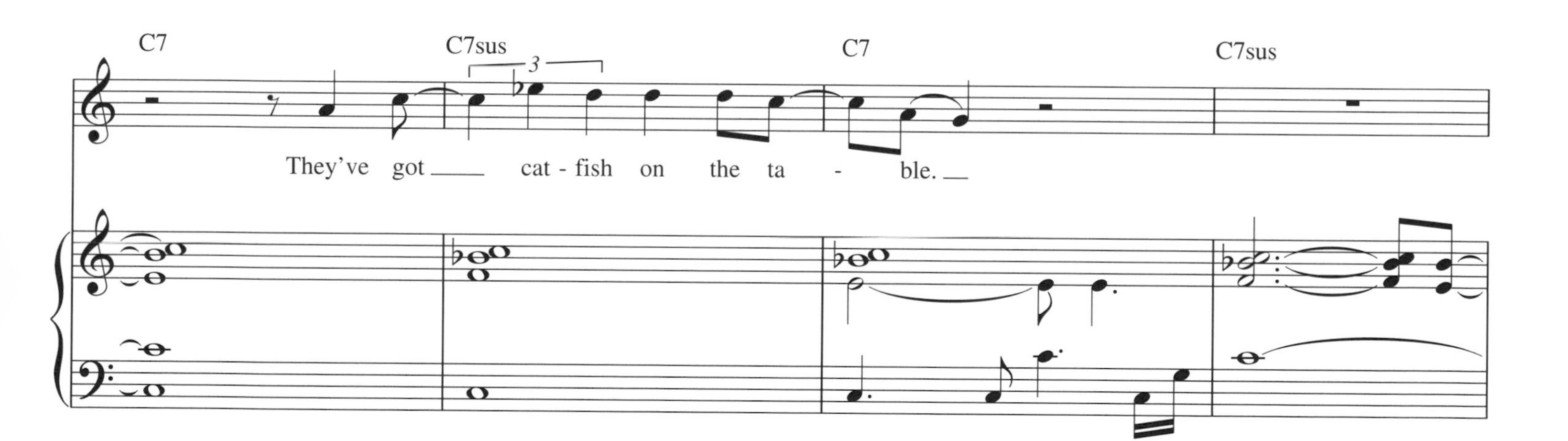
C7 C7sus C7 C7sus
3
They've got cat - fish on the ta - ble.

C7 C7sus C7 C7sus
They've got gos - pel in the air.
3

Freely
C7
E7
F7
And Rev - er - end Green be glad to see you when you
F♯dim7
G
F5
G5
C5
have - n't got a prayer, but boy, you've got a prayer in Mem - phis.
a tempo
mp
A5
F5
G5
C5
A5
F5
G5
C5
Now Mur - i - el plays pi - a - no
A5
F5
G5
C5
A5
F5
ev - 'ry Fri - day at the Hol - ly - wood, and

G5 C5 A5 F5 G5 C5
they brought me down to see her and they asked me if I would,
A5 F G5 C5 Am
would do a lit - tle num - ber and I
cresc.
mf
F G5 C Am F5 G7 C
sang with all my might. She said, "Tell me, are you a Chris -
Am F C
- tian, child?" and I said, "Ma'am, I am to - night." Walk-ing in Mem -

F G C Am F G C
-phis, I was walk-ing with my feet ten feet off of Beale.
Am F G C Am
Walk-ing in Mem - phis, but do I real-ly
F Em Dm7 C Am F G C
feel the way I feel? Walk - ing in Mem - phis,
Am F G C
I was walk-ing with my feet ten feet off of Beale.

Am F G C Am
Walk - ing in Mem - phis, but do I real - ly

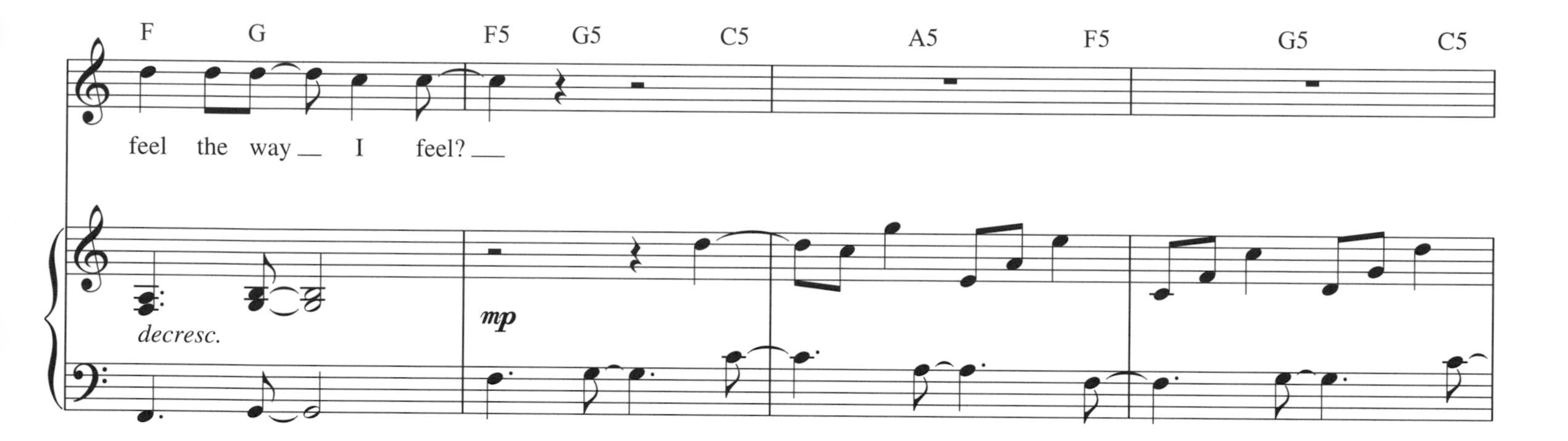
F G F5 G5 C5 A5 F5 G5 C5
feel the way I feel?
decresc.
mp

A5 F5 G5 C5 A5 F5
Put on my blue suede shoes and I

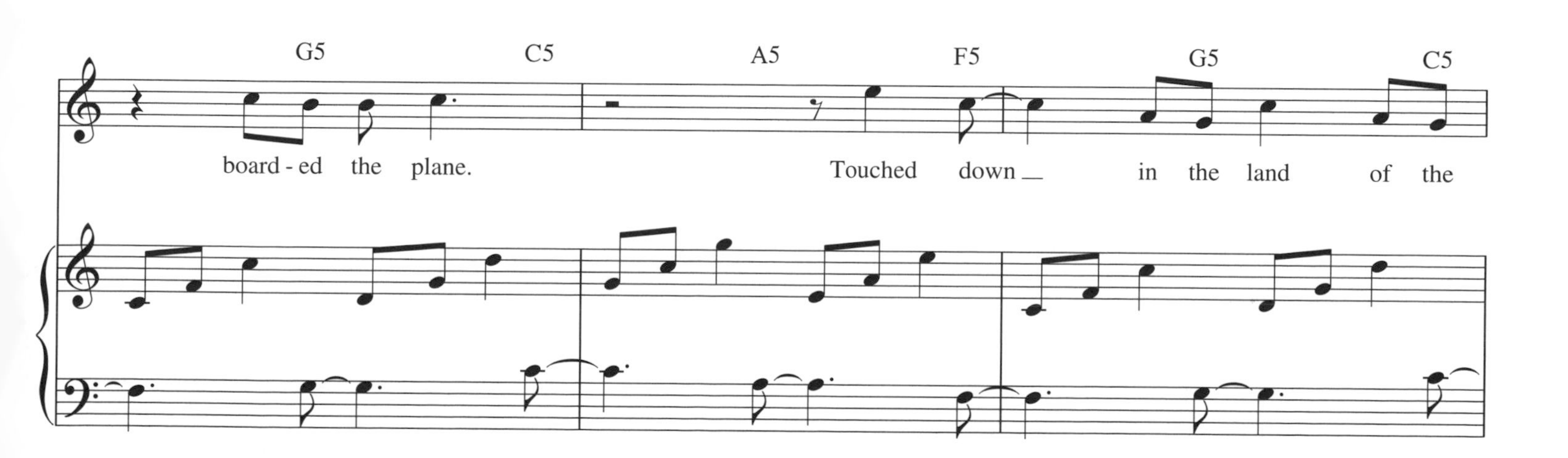
G5 C5 A5 F5 G5 C5
board - ed the plane. Touched down in the land of the

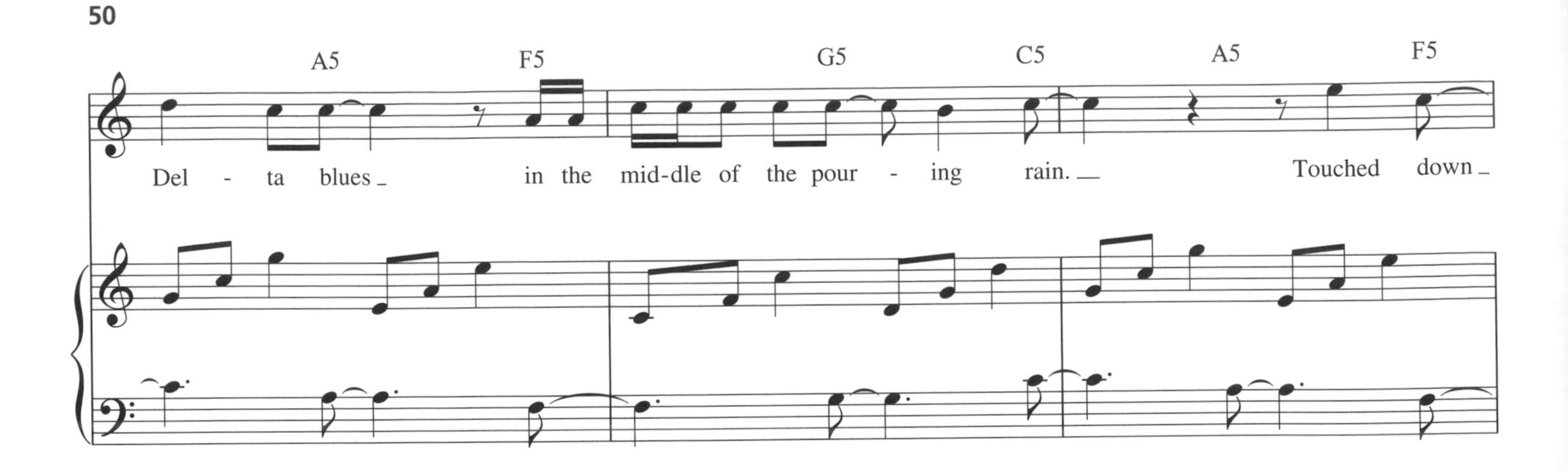
A5 F5 G5 C5 A5 F5
Del - ta blues in the mid-dle of the pour - ing rain.
Touched down

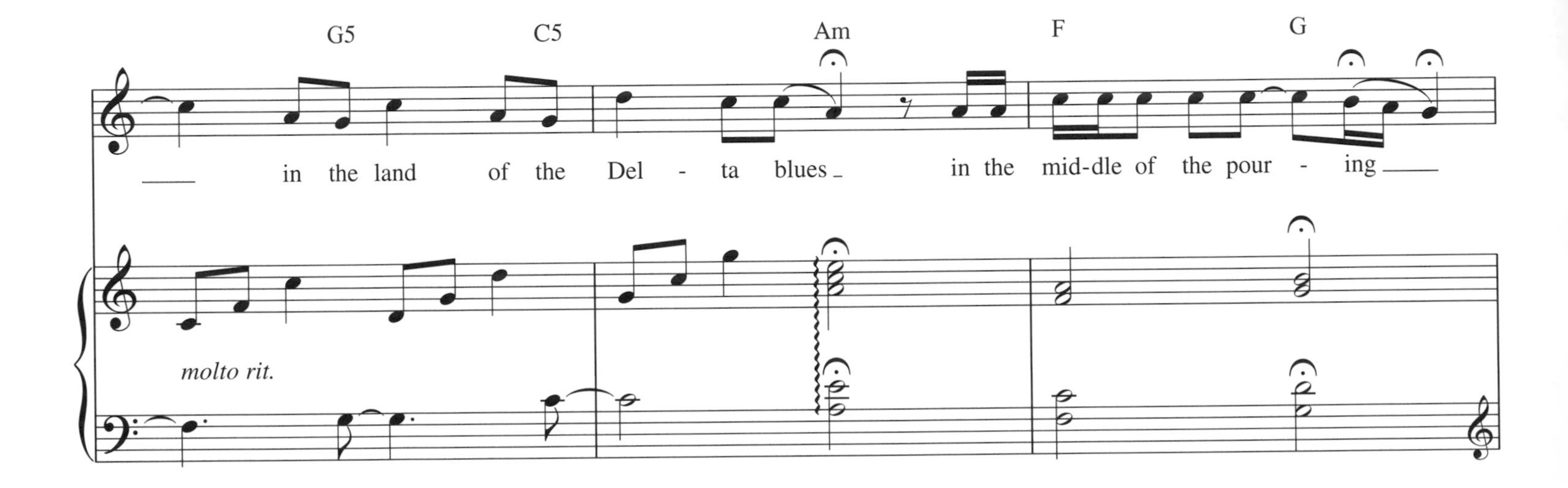
G5 C5 Am F G
in the land of the Del - ta blues in the mid-dle of the pour - ing
molto rit.

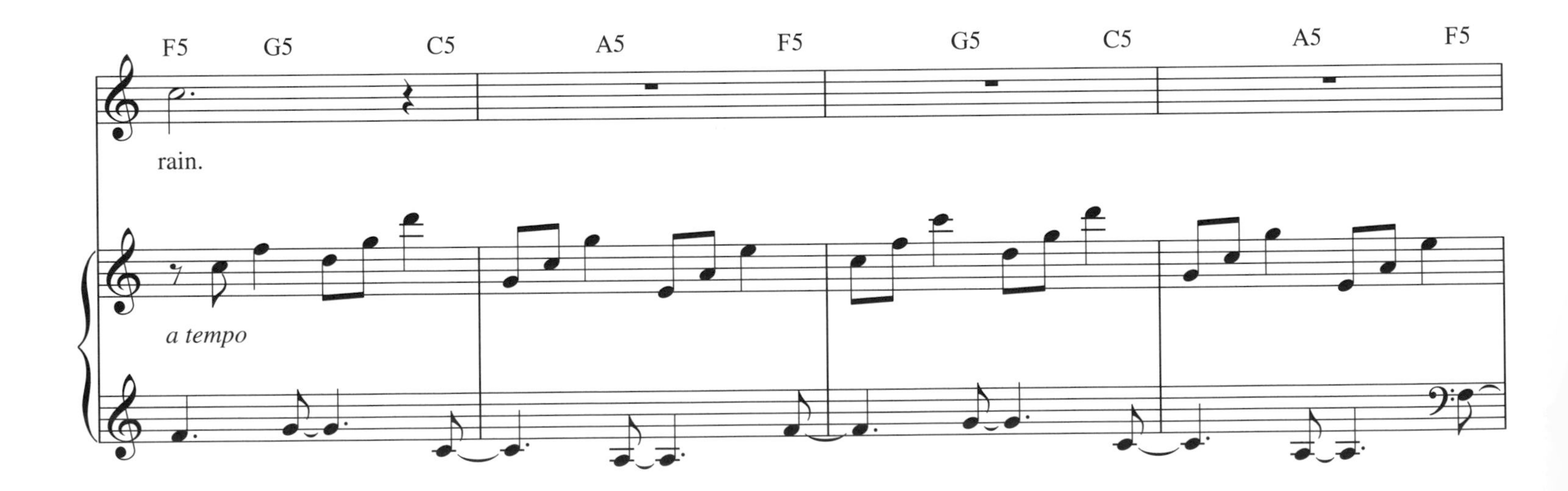
F5 G5 C5 A5 F5 G5 C5 A5 F5
rain.
a tempo

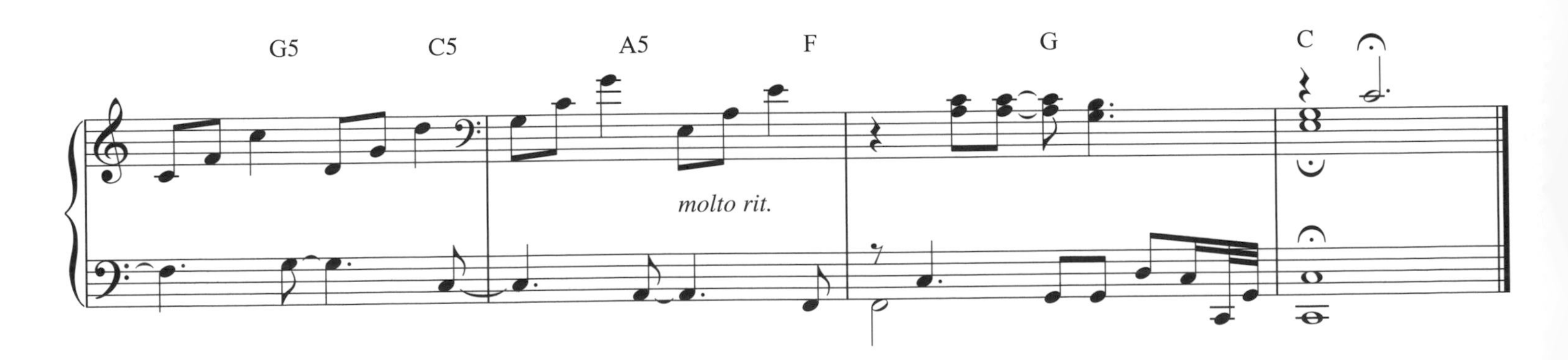
G5 C5 A5 F G C
molto rit.

What a Fool Believes

Words and Music by Michael McDonald
and Kenny Loggins

A9 Ab13sus Abb9/Gb Db/F
She mus-ters a smile for his nos - tal - gic tale.
some - where back in her long a - go,
Ebm7 Ab9sus Adim7 Bbm7 A9 Ab13sus Ab9/Gb Db/F
Nev - er com - in' near what he want - ed to say, on - ly to
where he can still be - lieve there's a place in her life. Some - day,
Ebm7 Ab9sus Adim7 Bbm7
re - al - ize it nev - er real - ly was.
some - where, she will re - turn.
Bbm7 A9b5 Ab13sus
She had a place in his life.

Bbm7
A9b5
He never made her think
Ab13sus
Ebm7
Ab9sus
Dbmaj7
twice. As he rises to her a-
B7
Bb7
Ebm7
Ab9sus
Bbm7
pology, anybody else would surely know
Gm7b5
F#m7
he's watching her go, but what a fool believes.

B9sus
he sees, no
E
B/D♯
wise man has the pow - er to rea - son a - way.
C♯m7
To Coda
A
E/G♯
F♯m7
What seems
B9sus
to be is al - ways bet - ter than noth -

E
B/D♯
C♯m7
ing, and noth-ing at all
A
D.S. al Coda
keeps send-ing him
CODA
A
E/G♯
F♯m7
What seems
(Lead vocal ad lib.) (If love can come, and
B9sus
to be is al-ways bet-ter than noth-
love can go, then why can't love pre-tend, oh, no?
E
B/D♯
C♯m7
ing, and noth-ing at all...
Ooh, got the pow-er. Oh, now.

Repeat and Fade

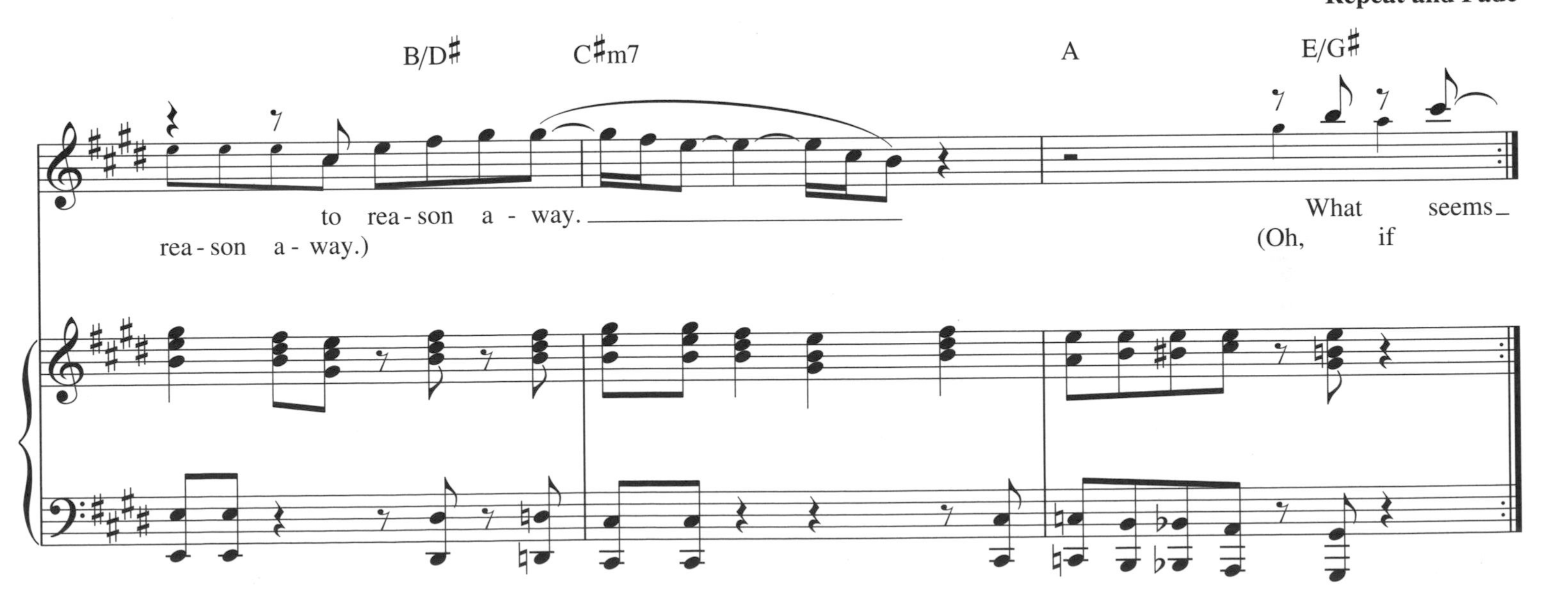